Praise for
Becoming a Soulful Parent

"*Becoming a Soulful Parent* is a beautiful, powerful, hands-on guide to parenting with a spiritual lens — with more intentionality, more presence, and with more wholeness. It is a wonderful companion in these difficult times."

— Rabbi Danya Ruttenberg, author of *Nurture the Wow*

Becoming a Soulful Parent is an open and non-judgmental window into the deepest truths that lie within the parenting landscape. Dasee Berkowitz's non-prescriptive approach embraces the creativity and resilience that is at the core of each family.

— Karina Zilberman, artist, educator, facilitator, and
  founder of the Shababa Approach to multigenerational
  Jewish experience.

Dasee Berkowitz helps us anchor (and calm) our roiling anxieties about the state of the world, while giving us the tools to shepherd our families through more personal, challenging terrain. With sensitivity, candor and humor, she guides us in how to strengthen our relationships through love, listening, empathy, curiosity and connection, while acknowledging how normal it is to feel like we're getting it wrong. *Becoming a Soulful Parent* is a perfect staple for every parent's bedside table.

— Abigail Pogrebin, author of *My Jewish Year: 18 Holidays,
  One Wondering Jew*

This book is a priceless, life-saving gift to every family at any time, but especially during days of challenge. You will find the best of yourself within its pages, guaranteed to spill over into your home and into the hearts of all those you love.

— Lori Palatnik, Author, International Speaker, and Founding Director of Momentum

Dasee Berkowitz illuminates new pathways not only into our souls, but into viewing the world, relationships and Jewish wisdom. She will support you and your ability to listen to your own voice and escort you to a time when the "real you shows up." With insightful questions she invites us to become more expansive to new images, insights and discoveries about ourselves and our roles as parents and family members that will bring a refreshingly new answer to the question *Ayeka?*, Where are you?

— Mark Horowitz, Vice President JCC Association North America

Becoming a Soulful Parent is an invitation to parents to explore our most important relationships, to get to know our kids and partners — and ourselves — better, and to grow in our becoming as families. Grounded in Judaic wisdom, but relevant to parents of all faith traditions, this book tackles such topics as sibling rivalry, marriage and coparenting, and nurturing relationships with grandparents. It's a guide for everyday parenting struggles and for parenting in a pandemic. The workbook prompts will help you go deeper in the best way. Make this your new nightly read — bring a pen or your phone to take notes and tell the family you're busy becoming better.

— Ellen O'Donnell, PhD, co-author of *Bless This Mess: A Modern Guide to Faith and Parenting in a Chaotic World*

BECOMING A SOULFUL PARENT

A path to the wisdom within

Dasee Berkowitz

Kasva Press

St. Paul / Alfei Menashe

While the stories related here are true, in a few cases names and identifying characteristics have been changed.

Book design & layout: Yael Shahar
Cover art: Susie Lubell
Author photo: Alisa Kotler-Berkowitz
Translations from the Hebrew Bible: Yael Shahar

First edition published 2021
Kasva Press LLC
www.kasvapress.com
Alfei Menashe, Israel / St. Paul, Minnesota
info@kasvapress.com

Becoming a Soulful Parent: A path to the wisdom within
ISBN
Paperback: 978-1-948403-19-1
Ebook: 978-1-948403-20-7

9 8 7 6 5 4 3 2 1

In memory of my mother,
Mozelle Berkowitz *z"l*
Your love is beyond measure and transcends worlds.

Contents

BECOMING A SOULFUL PARENT

A path to the wisdom within

Introduction
A Letter to the Reader

Dear Parent,

I bet we have a lot in common. If you are anything like me, you probably go to sleep exhausted every night, sometimes with a touch of anxiety, wondering if everyone will be okay the next day. You might have one child who is goofing off too much at school or one who is struggling to fit in. I sometimes feel like we all should get a standing ovation for how much we are balancing — family, work, self-care, and cultivating other relationships in our lives.

While we have a lot in common, we each have our own life story too. As for me, I live in Jerusalem with my husband and three kids and have been married for over a decade. Though I am writing from my heteronormative experience, there are so many ways to be a family — single parents by choice, same-sex couples, blended families. Whatever your family model, I think all of us parents have stories to tell, wisdom to give, and much to gain from sharing our parenting journeys with one another.

Becoming a Soulful Parent: A path to the wisdom within is a compilation of the wisdom I have absorbed over the past several years while directing Ayeka's Becoming a Soulful Parent program, an experience that enabled me to meet and learn from scores of talented people who have facilitated our parenting groups in synagogues, JCCs, and communities throughout North America. The book is guided by my learning first and foremost with these parents and educators. The inspiration for the book came from my mentor and colleague Rabbi Aryeh Ben David, founder of Ayeka, when we sat down several years ago to imagine what parents really need in a market saturated with parenting books, workshops, and podcasts.

This book is not only about my life but all of our lives.

You see, many other parenting approaches offer tips and tricks for how to be a better parent for your children. Some offer whole systems of behavior modification, with scripts and ideas for follow-through. I remember one participant in our Chicago group lamenting, "I have a stack of parenting books on my bedside table, but I find them so hard to use! Unless I follow the whole system, I feel like I can't do any of it." The books written by child development experts are well researched, but sometimes they leave us regular parents feeling deficient. When their approach doesn't work, you wonder what is wrong with your child...or what is wrong with you.

This book has a different agenda. There are no how-tos or systems of behavior modification to adopt. Each chapter contains a mix of personal anecdotes, insights from Jewish tradition and general culture, and an Ayeka Workbook section with reflective questions.

And while the book is replete with examples from Jewish wisdom, it is open to parents of all backgrounds.

The workbooks are the inner life of the book, and I hope they will help you discover insights about your life that you may not have given yourself the time or space to reflect upon. Consider writing down your responses to these questions or speak them aloud and discuss them with other parents. They are keys to opening windows into your inner life.

The questions we will be asking here are not the "Did you think of trying...?" or "Why don't you consider...?" variety. Those kinds of questions presume right and wrong ways of doing things. The kinds of questions I will pose will hopefully help you listen to your own voice, connect you with your intuitive wisdom, and lead you to your own answers. They start with "Consider..." and "Explore..." and "Imagine..." Open questions can reveal new possibilities. Open questions can help evoke the voice of your soul.

An anecdote about listening to your own voice: I love to sing and harmonize, and in 2018, I participated in a singing workshop.[1] As we were all standing in a circle and singing together, I realized I couldn't hear my voice. I needed to press my fingers into my ears so that I could block out the other participants' sound and hear my own. I understood that while I love to harmonize, it's easy to get lost in the chorus of voices and forget how to hear my unique contribution to the sound we are creating together.

As a parent, I sometimes experience that same sensation — getting lost in other people's music and forgetting my own. I get so swept up by other people's harmonies — what those parents are doing so well! — and overlook my own song.

There's a teaching by the Sefat Emet,[2] a Hasidic master from the nineteenth century, on the difference between speech (*dibur*) and voice (*kol*). With speech we can express ideas, feelings, and

---

1. The insights are gleaned from Dr. Elie Holtzer's singing workshop "Mizmor Shir L'Yom Hashabbat" on November 7, 2018.

2. Yehudah Aryeh Leib Alter (1847–1905), also known by the title of his main work, the *Sefat Emet* (Language of Truth), was a Hasidic rabbi who succeeded his grandfather, Rabbi Yitzchak Meir Alter, as the head of the rabbinical court and rav of Góra Kalwaria, Poland (known in Yiddish as the town of Ger).

practical communication. We say "Well done!" to a colleague and "I love you" to our children. We also say firm words such as "No, not now!" when we want to set a boundary. Speech is important. It allows us to communicate; it's efficient. But it can also be insufficient. Words alone cannot convey the fullness of what we want to express.

This is where *kol*, the voice, comes in. Speech is generic, but each person's voice is unique. If I close my eyes, I can hear my grandmother's voice, its tone and singsongy lilt. I can hear the voice of my younger daughter when she calls *"Imma!"* (Mommy) amid throngs of other children. Her voice is immediately recognizable; it's just *her*.

Our voice, says the Sefat Emet,[3] and the voice of those we love, is more than a thing to be cherished; it is redemptive. Only one voice sounds just like yours. Only one voice can sing your unique song.

This is true of your life on the whole — and certainly true of your life as a parent.

Your particular relationship with your family comes from a deep inner place and is expressed in a completely irreplaceable way.

Becoming a Soulful Parent: A path to the wisdom within will help you become attuned to your inner voice. Once you have mastered listening to that voice, this book will also guide you to better listen to your child's voice. How can you help each child listen to their own voice? How can you honor their unique contribution to your family? I hope that this book will help you answer these questions.

This book is not only about you and your children; it's about the whole package. In the chapters that follow, you'll find

---

3. Sefat Emet, Pesach 5633 on Exodus 14.

a wealth of spiritual practices — including prayer, Shabbat celebration, and the practice of connecting to our own inner spiritual resources — to help you connect with the totality of your experience as a parent.

If you are in a relationship, two chapters on partnership will guide you to appreciate your partner's inner voice. The chapter on grandparents is about connecting to time-honored wisdom and stories as an important element of raising your family.

In the chapter "Parenting through Difficult Times," you'll find spiritual practices that can help ground you, especially when concern, anxiety, and worry begin to surface.

Throughout this book I will repeatedly ask *Ayeka?* (Where are you?) with regard to the topic we are exploring. The question, I hope, will help you learn to listen to your own voice. Your answers will lead you to the next step.

You're a parent — you're busy. You don't need to read this book cover to cover. Pick it up and work with whichever chapter seems relevant to you now. Skip around. Let the questions percolate. Ask a friend, your partner, or a group of friends to help you reflect on the questions I ask in the workbook sections. When you are done, gather your family and reflect on the questions together. You will be amazed at what you discover.

Let's get started.

A Note on Strange Times

Parenting through a Pandemic

As I was ready to press Send on this manuscript, COVID-19 happened. As of this writing, we are six months into it. While we don't know when it will end, we know that at some point it will. It will also leave in its wake so much loss: the loss of the ones we love most and to whom we couldn't say a proper goodbye; the loss of jobs — so many jobs — that left us bereft of income and a sense of purpose; the loss of a sense of certainty, replaced by a sense that the world order as we have known it has changed.

COVID-19 brings with it an awareness that is unprecedented. We have become more aware of our own fragility, our common humanity, and the limitations on our human understanding of virology. While we are dependent on science and medicine to create a vaccine, we know deep down that COVID-19 is not the first, nor will it be the last, new virus to surface. There is so much we don't know.

It is also a time to appreciate so many things that we previously took for granted. Simple pleasures such as seeing a friend (at a distance of six feet!) or listening to the birds early in the morning can replenish our tired minds and bodies as many of us stay put, sheltering in place. The doctors, nurses, and all of the health-care professionals summon superpower strength to focus and care for the sick when the health-care system is overwhelmed with cases. Neighbors organize other community members to make sure food and medicine are delivered to those who are isolated, and we feel a renewed optimism that our concern for one another is stronger than our fear and indifference.

COVID-19 jolted us into a new way of being.

Some of us have reorganized our homes, work lives, and priorities to be able to homeschool our children for months on end. Some of us have to work harder than ever to keep our jobs, juggling between professional demands and our children's need for attention. Some of us feel crushed and depleted; the everyday demands are overwhelming.

Those of us who have lost our jobs or are furloughed experience open expanses of time with our children that we are not used to. We spend days exploring the outdoors, painting, baking, and biking. We spend other days feeling anxious and full of dread, not quite ready to be thrust into the role of full-time parent.

While speaking to other parents, two main kinds of questions come up again and again:

When will we get back to life as we knew it?

What are we looking forward to once COVID-19 passes?

There are two different attitudes toward these kinds of questions. The first looks backward, while the other looks forward. The questions are like a study in basic grammar: We are happy to long for the past tense or hope toward the future; it's the present tense we don't want to inhabit. But the impulse to ask these questions is absolutely clear. It comes from an attitude of "Get me out of here!!!"

There is another way. Instead of trying to escape the present, we can adopt a *becoming* mindset. The tense of *becoming* is *present continuous*. We move through a period of time and become transformed by it. Difficult times are never things that we can sidestep, ignore, or deny. They need to be moved *through*. While parenting through the pandemic, the questions that guide me are: *How* am I going to move through this time? What are the internal resources I can depend on? When do I need to exercise more self-compassion? And how can I help my children access their own internal resources as well?

In the chapters that follow, we will focus on cultivating a becoming mindset and how connecting to our inner spiritual resources can guide us during this and inevitably other trying times we face as parents and as people.

After a vaccine against COVID-19 has been created, we will all be able to breathe more easily. But we will emerge forever changed.

1

Beyond a Management Mindset

Your Child Has a Purpose

I am starting to believe in divine grace — or in lay terminology, the possibility for change. Lately there has been a growing distance between my son and everyone around him. His elementary school English teacher keeps asking me, "Is everything okay?" His beloved math teacher took him aside: "You are a student who can achieve 100 percent, but you disrupt the class too much." His father and I have repeatedly questioned him (mostly under our breath), "What's going on?" And sometimes at night, under the layers of down comforters, we have whispered worriedly, "Do you think we are losing him?"

We aren't crazy about his friends and we only feel close to a few parents of kids in his grade. Naturally, we started to question whether we are sending him to the right school; we want him to have better influences. Usually my instinct is to "wait and see." But this approach is questionable. What if there really are behaviors that won't change without our intervention? What if the window is closing on making a difference in his life, and we are going to miss it?

And yet, even during this uncertain stage, we have experienced moments of divine grace, of closeness, of *finding him* again. In those moments when he gets angry because he's frustrated, his soft, vulnerable side emerges, searching to connect: "I get lonely sometimes. Can you keep me company?" Or when he climbed into my bed the other night to ask me about a bump on his face that is not going away (his first pimple, as it turns out), I could now teach him how to wash his face with soap.

When my son begins a sentence with "Imma, can you please..." I feel a drop of divine grace falling on me, a reminder of his call to connect and my call to answer.

Ego Stories and Soul Stories

The renowned writer, activist, and educational reformer Parker J. Palmer, together with his colleague at the Center for Courage and Renewal, Marcy Jackson, writes about two narratives that are running through our minds all of the time: our ego stories and our soul stories.[1] Our ego stories star in the "curated Me" — you know, the self I present at dinner parties or invite to my interviews. The curated Me is linear, with an upward and forward trajectory. The narratives we tell when we are speaking from a place of *ego* focus on life's high points and the times when we have been successful and affirmed. They focus on *my* story; I am *the* story. When something throws me off track, my *ego voice* (the one telling my ego story) becomes reactive and defensive.

Soul stories, on the other hand, honor the shadow as well as the light. They notice the suffering as much as the gladness.

1. Parker Palmer and Marcy Jackson, "Ego Stories & Soul Stories," worksheet from Courage to Lead, accessed September 23, 2019, https://www.clearpathcounsel.com/files/4313/3029/8683/Ego_Stories__Soul_Stories.pdf.

These are the stories that keep us up at night. They allow us to integrate fragments and inconsistency within the whole. As Palmer writes, soul stories are not afraid of fear, loss, failure, or mystery. They are the stories that fold into a larger story. Instead of saying, "I am *the story*," we can say, "I am a part of *a larger story*." When something throws us off track, our soul voice soothes us and reminds us, "Throughout your story, you will experience many ups and downs. At some point, you will feel those parts working together, creating wholeness. Right now that moment might feel far away. But have faith, it will come." Once I was exposed to the concept of ego stories and soul stories, I slowly became more attuned to what is happening inside my head, especially during interactions with my kids.

My ego voice screams, "Why can't you be like other kids? *Other* parents aren't getting calls every evening from the teacher sharing the latest behavioral mess-up of the day. What's *wrong* here?"

My soul voice speaks with more understanding. "This is what my child is experiencing *now*. We moved to Israel a few years ago. My son is a new immigrant in a new school. He is trying to figure out how to fit in." Beyond empathy, my soul voice takes me a drop deeper, saying, "He has a soul too. Sometimes he follows the rules and does what we expect of him, and sometimes he doesn't. He's creative, strong-willed, and determined. The way he is acting is how his creativity, will, and determination are expressing themselves. There is nothing wrong here. These core qualities of his will develop and become refined throughout his life. This *is* him. Love him — *all* of him."

Our soul voices soothe us; our ego voices keep us on edge.

My ego voice is on high volume most of the time. I think that might be true for a lot of us today. We are bombarded by digital media showing us the picture-perfect way to be a family.

We are surrounded by external measurements of success, and our anxiety about our children's employability in the competitive job market of the future grows daily. Small talk with other parents, while collecting the kids from school or at the playground, raises our anxiety level even higher — "Your child hasn't mastered conversational Chinese yet? Don't worry, it will come" [with patronizing smile]. These voices and encounters are valuable when they help us create opportunities for our children to compete and succeed in the world. But they might not serve us all the time. When I am trying to cultivate a closer, more soulful connection in my family, it serves me to turn down the ego voice and turn up my soul voice.

Soul Meeting Soul

Parker J. Palmer once wrote that the process of education is the condition of the teacher's soul meeting the condition of the student's soul.

> Face to face with my students, only one resource is at my immediate command: my identity, my selfhood, my sense of this "I" who teaches — without which I have no sense of the "Thou" who learns.[2]

I wonder if it's like that in our families too. The condition of each of our inner lives plays out in our family dynamics. When we clash, it's my ego voice against my son's: my *need* for him to live up to my expectations versus his *need* to "be himself" at all costs.

But what if I consciously enable a soul-to-soul connection instead?

---

2. Parker J. Palmer, *Courage to Teach: Exploring the Inner Landscape of a Teacher's Life* (San Francisco: Jossey-Bass, 1997).

My son is different from me. I am much more interested in spiritual matters than practical ones. I would rather gaze at a flower; he would prefer to build, dismantle, and rebuild his desk. My idea of a good time is sitting with a friend and talking about my feelings all day long. His is figuring out how to build a fire with a match and some twigs.

A soul-to-soul connection is one in which I appreciate that his daring, cleverness, and strong-mindedness, together with the parts of his soul that are searching and open for connection, *make him who he is*. Though it is easier to rejoice when my son is a mini-me, I need to appreciate when my son is a *right-sized him*. This realization can open the channel for soul-to-soul connection between us, but it is conscious, hard work (to say the least!) to maintain this mindset during all of our interactions.

The Talmud (Niddah 31a) relates, "There are three partners in a human being: the Holy One, the father, and the mother." While parents might bequeath part of the "raw material" in the creation of a human being, it is the Holy One who gives children all the good stuff. God, or the "Third Partner," gives each child "the spirit and the breath, beauty of features, eyesight, the power of hearing and the ability to speak and to walk, understanding and discernment." In short, the Third Partner provides all of what makes our children who they are. Kahlil Gibran relates that our children are not ours. Instead,

They are the sons and daughters of Life's longing for itself . . .

You may house their bodies but not their souls

For their souls dwell in the house of tomorrow, which you cannot visit, not even in your dreams.[3]

---

3. Kahlil Gibran, *The Prophet* (New York: Penguin Books, 2019), 19–22.

Our children are not just like us. They are just like *them*. They are meant to be exactly as they are.

Asking, *Ayeka?*

Sometimes our "management mindset" gets in the way. A management mindset is the one that is busy making lists. "Call the math teacher to improve my child's basic computing skills", "make sure to sign-up for dance class", "remember to reassign the chores on the chore wheel so that my child cultivates a work ethic!" So many of us are preoccupied by managing our children and their lives that we don't take the time to reflect on the parents we want to become. Sometimes we need help remembering to make the shift.

To start to become attuned to your ego voice and your soul voice and how they play into your relationships, ask yourself, *Ayeka?* (Where are you?) More specifically, where are you in your relationship with your family?

Asking *Ayeka?* isn't about your physical location. It originates from the Hebrew Bible, where it is the first question ever asked. After Adam eats the fruit that God had expressly forbidden eating, Adam hides "among the trees" in the Garden of Eden and God calls out *"Ayeka?"* (Genesis 3:8). Clearly the omniscient God knows where Adam is hiding and isn't asking about Adam's physical location. God is asking about the condition of Adam's soul. It's a version of "Is this your best? Have you shown yourself worthy of being in the Garden of Eden?"

Rav Abraham Isaac Kook, the chief rabbi of British Mandatory Palestine, says that Adam didn't know how to answer the question "Where are you?" because he was estranged from his true self. "[Adam] lost touch with his true 'I'-ness, his truest self."[4] Only when we can create a pathway to access our authentic "I" will we be able to find our way back when we lose our way.

When we are faced with challenges in our families — whether we feel a growing distance between members of our family or we don't appreciate our children or our partners — the only thing we have the power to change is ourselves. We can change either how we *understand* the situation or how we *respond* to it. In other words, when confronting a challenge and before choosing a course of action, we can first ask ourselves, "How can I journey toward my own truest 'I'?"

That journey begins with an openness to ask ourselves vulnerable questions, the patience and humility to hear the answers that emerge, and the courage to act on those answers. As the journalist and author Krista Tippett reflects, the right kind of question — when met honestly and openly — can be redemptive.[5] It can build us in ways we didn't think were possible.

Open questions are very different from closed questions. As parents, we know how closed questions can shut down the hope for growth and change. "Why didn't you do X?" "How could you have done Y?" Open and generous questions, however, can suddenly encourage us to imagine growth. "Tell me more about X?" or "How are you thinking/feeling about Y now?"

Four pivotal Ayeka questions will keep coming up throughout this book in different forms. While each section's questions might be phrased slightly differently, here is the heart of the questions we will be asking:

---

4. Abraham Isaac Kook, *Orot HaKodesh* (Jerusalem: Mossad HaRav Kook, 1990), 3:140.

5. Krista Tippett, *Becoming Wise: An Inquiry into the Mystery and Art of Living* (New York: Penguin Press, 2016), 30.

Where am I (given an issue or question)?

How do I want to grow?

What obstacles get in my way?

What's a small step I can take toward moving forward?

Our honest answers to these questions can help us become the parents we want to be. They can help us move from a management mindset to a more reflective one, from a "fixed mindset" to a "growth mindset." Psychologist Carol Dweck defines a fixed mindset as one where people believe their basic qualities, such as intelligence or talent, are simply fixed traits. In a growth mindset, people believe that their most basic abilities can be developed through dedication and hard work — brains and talent are just the starting point.[6] Such an attitude creates a love of learning and a resilience that is essential for a meaningful life.

A fixed mindset is the hallmark of relationships on autopilot. To someone with a fixed mindset, any challenging question would be met with the resigned, stagnant answer: this is how it is. Asking the four Ayeka questions can spur us toward a growth mindset — one in which we acknowledge the potential for change.

---

6. Carol S. Dweck, *Mindset: The New Psychology of Success* (New York: Random House, 2016).

Ayeka Workbook

Take out a notebook and pen and write down your answers to the following questions.[7] Give yourself some time; five to eight minutes is good for a start. Write freely and don't censor yourself. When you feel as though you are finished writing, write some more. More truth comes out the second time around.

> *Where am I — Ayeka? — in parenting my child right now? What am I proud of and where am I stuck?*

> *What is one way I want to move forward as a parent to my child?*

> *What is an obstacle that gets in my way?*

> *What is one practical piece of advice my soul voice would give me in order to move past the obstacle?*

Sometimes We Expect Too Much

The other day, I returned from a meeting that exhausted me. The nervous energy of the man I was meeting with was electric. He spoke about a crisis, about brokenness and the need for a serious intervention. He is becoming the resource

---

7. Today's families range in size, in most of the Ayeka Workbook sections, I refer to 'your child'. If you have more than one child, you are welcome to change your reading accordingly.

in a community of parents whose children are not "living up to" their parents' expectations of them — children whose actions today are slaps in their parents' faces. The parents feel lost — "I thought that if only I raised them with X values, they would turn out with an X lifestyle." Of course, we know — cognitively — that human development and growth never add up in a neat formula, and yet so many parents of grown children find themselves feeling this way. The younger generation's decisions to violate their parents' deeply held beliefs bring pain, confusion, and estrangement between the two generations.

We cannot control or predict what will happen with our children. We can only provide the right conditions for growth and be witness to their development. We all want our children to grow into the authentic selves they were meant to be, for their souls to find their destiny and bring their unique *tikkun* (repair) to a broken world. It all sounds good in theory...But all too often, we get in our own way of that happening.

Ayeka Workbook

) *Share a time when your child made a different choice from you about a significant issue. How did you react?*

) *Listen to your soul voice. How does it guide you to react?*

) *Listen for your child's soul voice. What do they need from you?*

Over the last couple of years, I have started a new ritual. At the end of every day, I tell my kids about their "good inner point" (*nekudah tovah*), a teaching from Rebbe Nachman of Breslov, the founder of the Breslov Hasidic movement.[8] I tell them about the moments, big and small, that I noticed when they behaved in beautiful, life-affirming ways; when I heard their soul voices coming through. It's a simple reflective practice. It channels my aspiration to appreciate my children more, and it responds to their need to *feel* my appreciation and love for them more. Sometimes they will tell me what my *nekudah tovah* was: "You didn't yell at us so much today!" Turns out, they can discern what was good in me that day too.

---

8. Rebbe Nachman of Breslov, *Likkutei Moharan* 282.

2
Being Ourselves
You Are the Parent
Your Child Needs

I don't like crying in public. It's awkward, especially when I don't have a tissue nearby. Some kinds of public are okay, such as the movies or synagogue, or at funerals. But other times are decidedly not okay, such as the times when I am called to the head teacher's office to deal with my child's behavioral problem. Definitely not then.

I sat in the small meeting room (the size of a closet) with my daughter Shalva and her kindergarten teacher, Shulamit. The teacher was delivering a stern message about the unacceptable way my daughter had acted the day before — disrespectful and wild, to put it mildly. While her teacher was speaking, my daughter was squirming and writhing in her chair. She was nervous, upset, and serious in a way I hadn't seen my little firecracker before.

The strict speech from Shulamit was necessary and clear, but unrelenting. In those fifteen minutes, my face became damp with tears. It was hard to see my child so uncomfortable. When the conversation ended and the consequences levied, Shalva's teacher told her it was over and said, "Go and play."

Shalva didn't want to play — she wanted to collapse in my arms in a heap. And that's what she did.

Her teacher approached me a few minutes later. "I saw that it was hard for you too," she said. I felt embarrassed to admit that it was. The meeting was hard for me because I felt as though a strict judgment had been delivered without the softening agent of love. And yet, it was very effective. Shalva's behavior in the classroom is decidedly improving.

Since that encounter, I have attempted to instruct myself, "Be the kindergarten teacher!" If only I could command the same level of respect and clearheaded discipline at home. The day after the meeting at school, I found myself copying the kindergarten teacher's approach: *Channel your inner Shulamit.*

But I'm not Shulamit; I'm me. And while I may be able to *learn* from her approach, I ultimately need to find and refine my own. As we all do. My daughter doesn't need another Shulamit; she needs me to be me.

We Are the Parents Our Children Need

There's a beautiful teaching from the first word of the third book of the Bible, Leviticus. The word is *vayikra* — literally, "He called."[1] It's from the Hebrew root *kuf-reish-alef*, which is also the root of the words meaning "call" and "to be called." A similar sounding word in Hebrew has a very different meaning — *karah*, meaning "happened," with the Hebrew root *kuf-reish-hey*. This root also gives us *b'mikreh*, which means "accidental" or "by happenstance." Without going too deep into whether you believe in the randomness of all things or whether your worldview is

---

1. "He" refers to God.

more deterministic, in our day-to-day lives, it's easy to think most things happen by coincidence: "I just happened to bump into that friend at the market who told me to take that class" or "I just happened to take that left turn and get stuck in a traffic jam."

When we think that everything is random, it's easy to rejoice: "I'm so happy I got to take that class. What a coincidence that I ran into my friend at just that time!" Or complain: "I can't believe I took that left turn. I am going to be in this car now for hours!"

When we shift our perspective from *karah* (it just happened) to *kara* (I was called on), every situation becomes an opportunity to respond. The question shifts from one that reflects the randomness of life — "How am I so lucky?" or "Why do I have such bad luck?" — to "What meaning can I make of this joyful or unfortunate situation?" Or more specifically, "What am I *called* on to do in this moment, now that I am here?"

What if we applied the question to our children, both when things are going well at home *and* when we are all having a hard time? Do we say, "What luck! Everything is going so well right now, I just don't want anything to change!" In the opposite situation, do we question with exasperation, "Just my luck! Why is *my* child acting like this when everyone else's children seem to be doing just fine?!"

Instead, if we're focused on the wider perspective, we can ask ourselves, "Is it just *b'mikreh* (by accident) that I happen to be the parent to this particular child? Or is there more to it?"

When we ask this question, we open ourselves up to growth. "Perhaps this is the child I need in order to grow as a parent. Perhaps I am the parent my child needs to grow too."

Being Shulamit won't be much help now. Being Imma Dasee will.

Put a different way, you are the perfect parent for your child. I first heard that statement at our first Becoming a Soulful Parent workshop. What? With all of our foibles and ways in which we don't measure up? How could it be that *I'm* the *perfect parent* for my child? But once Aryeh Ben David, founder of Ayeka and our facilitator that evening, shared this sentence, we all felt a shift in the room. We are perfect, not in the sense that we never need to change or grow but rather that all the struggles and concerns we have about parenting are custom designed to help us become better human beings and parents. Our foibles may also be designed to help each of our children grow too.

"Beloved Is a Human Being"

"Beloved is a human being for being created in the image of God" begins the Mishnah in Pirkei Avot (3:14). We can interpret this verse to mean that we are created by *more* than just our genetic makeup. If all humans are created in the image of God, then each person is unique and infinitely valuable, with their own special divine stamp.

Presumably, it's fairly easy for us to apply this idea to our own children. Of course *they* are unique. My son strums the guitar in his particular way, and my daughter has a way of swallowing deeply before saying something important.

If we can internalize that our children are each unique, we should be able to see ourselves in the same light: infinitely unique, infinitely special. Sometimes we tend to forget that. I remember a participant in one of our Becoming a Soulful Parent groups who had never thought about what makes her unique or special, especially in how she raises her children. It's much easier to look at our friends or our kids' teachers or coaches and say, "Oh! Now that is good discipline. I should be more like her!" or "Oh! Look at how *that* father feeds his kids alfalfa sprouts. I wish I were more like him!"

Pirkei Avot 3:14 continues, "Humankind is more beloved still in that we are aware of being created in the image of God." I might *forget* that I have unique qualities — the precise qualities I need in order to be the best parent for the children I have. But with the *knowledge* of being created in the image of God, I am starting from a different place, one with a lot more self-appreciation.

Ayeka Workbook

 Write down three to five qualities that are just you. Choose the qualities that you really appreciate in particular. These might be qualities with which people describe you or qualities that only you know about.

 Circle a couple of those qualities. Elaborate on times when you feel as though you really embodied those qualities with your child.

What is one step you can take to remind yourself of those qualities, especially when things are challenging at home?

I took a turn at answering these questions. I feel that some of my *soul qualities* include being fun-loving, playful, flexible, and calm. Of those, I appreciate the calm quality the most. When things start getting hectic at home, and one of my kids is overly anxious about an assignment for school that was misplaced, or a squabble is beginning between one of my kids and a friend, I start to chant to myself and to my immediate surrounding, "It's okay, it's okay." And then I say, "Let's take a deep breath and slow things down a bit so that we can think clearly." My kids sometimes mock me for this deep-breathing business (and start to deep-breathe very rapidly, which quickly turns into hyperventilating). But I know that this calming presence is exactly what they need when things start whipping up into a frenzy. I am proud of myself that I can give that to them.

While we need to honor, celebrate, and pour loads of glitter all over our list of God-given amazing soul qualities as parents, let's also unpack the shadow side — the darker qualities that we also carry around with us — to be more aware of the obstacles we are facing in this journey.

Our Shadow Sides

Notwithstanding the triumphant moments I described above, there are times when I am not at all calm. There are times when I am scattered, or I lose it, and it is hard for me to calm *myself.* There are times when I forget to breathe. In these moments, my inner noise drowns out the "still small voice"[2] of my soul. I start to react impulsively and become unable to access the

---

2. The "still small voice" (*kol d'mamah daka*) — literally translated as "the voice of a tiny silence" — is a reference to 1 Kings 19:12 and portrays the dramatic meeting between Elijah the prophet and God.

quality of calm that I cherish.

It all starts out relatively benign. We are late for *this*, we have to rush to get *there*, or my evening conference call starts *in five minutes, please just go to sleep!* Especially for my little one, moving quickly and transitioning does not come easily. In short, as journalist and writer Krista Tippett likes to say, we can experience time as a bully.[3] And I don't always react so well when I feel bullied. In fact, I sometimes take it out on my kids.

I get impatient. I stand stiff with my arms folded. I feel tight inside. Understanding the root of the word *patience* offers me perspective and helps me understand what stands at the core of my feelings. *Savlanut*, the Hebrew word for "patience," comes from the Hebrew root *samekh-vet-lamed*, which can mean "to carry" (as in, to carry a heavy load). It also can mean "to suffer." When we are patient, we also suffer a little bit inside.

Patience, Where Are You?

There is another dimension to impatience. When I become impatient, it's because I feel unheard, unseen . . . unimportant. The great irony is that, when I start speaking sternly to my children from impatience, the situation I want to influence usually gets derailed and significantly more dramatic. Though in theory I know very well that impatience will only distance me from my big-picture goal, it is extremely hard to think so clearly in the moment of truth.

If my *soul voice* is calm, then it's my *ego voice* that is impatient. My ego voice says, "Hey, kids! You're not going according to

---

3. Interview with John O'Donohue and Krista Tippett, "The Inner Landscape of Beauty," *On Being*, last updated August 31, 2017, https://onbeing.org/programs/john-odonohue-the-inner-landscape -of-beauty-aug2017/.

my schedule! I am the center of the world here. Can you please get to it?" When I actively cultivate patience, I recognize that my kids are different from me. They are not as fast, experienced, or as skilled as I am. (I've had thirty-five more years than they've had to develop these capacities.) In the words of my mentor, Karina Zilberman, becoming patient moves me out of an "ego-system" where I am at the center and into an "ecosystem" in which we are all interconnected.

There is a Talmudic story (Shabbat 31a) that brings this message home. One Friday afternoon — pre-Shabbat "crunch time" for the rabbis! — two students make a bet: Who will be able to anger Hillel the Elder? They knock on Hillel's door while he is taking a bath. He emerges from the bath, throws on a robe, and answers the door. The students ask the rabbi one inane question after the next: "Why are the heads of the Babylonians oval?" "Why are the eyes of the residents of Tadmor bleary?" They had agreed that the first one to successfully aggravate Hillel would win a fistful of money (400 zuz). Hillel, however, answers each question calmly, even complimenting the students on the wise questions they ask.

I sometimes wonder if I could hear my own "Hillel the Elder" voice during my crunch times. Is it really so critical that my children brush their teeth that morning, or if they are five minutes late for school? (Of course, routines are important, but does it *really* matter if they get off schedule once in a while?) When I am impatient, I am responding to the granular detail of our lives and the urgency of the moment. I am focused on accomplishing each task at *all costs*. Strengthening my "patient muscle" helps me hear that calm soul voice a bit more. My children, like Hillel's students, would benefit.

Ayeka
Workbook

 What is the "noise" that drowns out your soul voice (those unique qualities that are just you)?

 Name one or two negative qualities that overtake the positive ones you named earlier.

 What new perspective would you like to bring to those qualities?

 What's one step you can take toward cultivating that perspective?

Until the Real Parent Shows Up

There's a saying that a therapist will use technique until the real therapist shows up. All the lessons learned and books read in graduate school will bolster a new therapist's confidence as they get started. The therapist will rely on their accumulated wisdom until a deeper wisdom sets in, an intuitive wisdom, the embodiment of the role that they now carry.

The same is true for parents. We read books about how we should discipline our children. We listen to podcasts about the importance of boundaries. Tips and tricks on getting our kids to listen are shared widely by parenting groups. I use them, I rely on them, I recommend them.

I do all of that . . . until the real mother shows up — the mother who has internalized the title she carries.

There is nothing like being in touch with an older generation of parents to remember how important this kind of embodied parenting is — the kind of parenting that is connected to intuitive wisdom. The day-to-day, moment-to-moment reality of parenting doesn't allow for the long view. Only our parents, our grandparents, or the elders in our communities can give us this perspective. Speaking to them is like an extended inhale that gives oxygen and expanse to our inner cavity.

I thought about this while looking through old photo albums in the living room of my childhood home. There I saw pictures of sassy me at age eight, adventurous me at age ten, and angry teenage me at age fifteen. While flipping through the pictures, I remembered how I felt at each age. Above all, I felt how much I am my parents' child, a thread in the tapestry of an extended family that unfolds and extends beyond my reach.

This perspective, this grounding, was helpful for me, especially a week later when I returned home to my nuclear family. I reconnected with my sassy daughter who takes my instructions as suggestions. I reconnected with my adventurous son who struts his independence like a badge of honor, dismissing his need for *us*, as any healthy preadolescent would. Once, I said to him, "Tamir, I will be the most important woman in your life." (Short of a love interest he may have later on.) He looked at me, a bit taken aback. Having surprised myself with the statement, I was taken aback too. I felt it to be true in a very full and embodied way. Any concerns about "losing him" gave way to a broader perspective. We will forever be interconnected. Together, this kind of knowing and my declarative statement expressed something true. Our children need to be held. They need to know that even when they try to push us away, we will still be there. And as their mom, I will continue to search for the ways in which I can strengthen my own soul qualities so that I can grow into becoming just the mother they need.

Embodied, intuitive, and reflective parenting happens only when we don't ever try to be another kind of parent — not the kindergarten teacher kind, nor the soccer coach kind, nor the one who feeds his kids alfalfa sprouts. Just *our* kind.

Ayeka Workbook

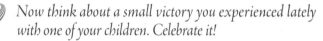

Think about a dilemma that you now face with one of your children. How does your soul voice inform your response to them?

What gets in the way of you responding in this way?

Now think about a small victory you experienced lately with one of your children. Celebrate it!

3

Relationships
More Than Just the Two of You

My husband, Leon, and I very rarely get a moment to ourselves. Children's calls of *"Imma! Abba* (Dad)!" punctuate almost all of our conversations. Interruptions are the air we breathe. In turn, we sometimes switch to autopilot when we relate to each other. Perhaps this is a natural coping mechanism to stave off feelings of disappointment and lack of connection. The thing is, autopilot won't help us chart new territory or soar to new heights. As the daily grind of family life keeps our gaze locked low, *soaring* and *heights* are words that vaguely recall an earlier period of our relationship.

One morning I was feeling extremely irked by the distance between us, which had lately been made worse by a hefty helping of arguments about one thing or another. I missed the spontaneity, laughter, and excitement that characterized our earlier years together (the reason we decided to start this company called our family in the first place). And so I began to offer my husband superficial and polite answers to any questions he asked me. Only later that morning, when we were sitting around the kitchen table finishing breakfast, did I reveal my technique. "Sweetheart, I have decided to treat you like a coworker. Coworkers are always cordial to one another." He laughed gently and nodded. "And furthermore," I continued, "I think the senior management of Berkowitz-Morris LTD is in desperate need of a team-building retreat."

After many weeks of trying to find time in our calendars to even look at the calendar, we settled on a date. Very kind and generous friends took our three children for the weekend. Before we left, I turned to our children and told them, half demanding, half cheerleading, "You are a team — take care of one another." I passed off the mantle of responsibility to them so that I could feel relieved from the burden of carrying it myself. My son gave me one of the longest hugs I can remember. "We aren't neglecting them," I reminded my husband as we descended the hills of Jerusalem — a city of stone and memory; majestic, often maddening, and the deep anchor of our lives during the past several years since moving to Israel. "We are giving them an adventure."

The road widened near Latrun, opening up to the lush green of early spring. The Mediterranean Sea was nearby. Its expansiveness invited me to expand too. In the first few moments of being alone together, I found that I couldn't stop talking. There were so many thoughts running through my head — encounters throughout my week, questions big and small, and stories about the kids. It was like a faucet, shut tight, had suddenly been opened. A day later, as our weekend drew to a close, I offered a prayer: "May we always remember how easy it can be to open channels that are closed between us."

Are Our Marriages on Autopilot?

So many of us take our partners for granted. We spend a lot of time and mental energy investing in people whom we don't really know or for whom we don't care deeply — from new acquaintances to colleagues at work. Jewish philosopher Martin Buber has a term for these kinds of relationships: I-It.[1] We treat the other person like an "it," someone who is there to help us move our lives forward, accomplish a simple task, or get ahead at work. These kinds of relationships are utilitarian. We often show our "best self" in specifically the "I-It" type of relationship. We are kind, polite, and pleasant.

Our sacred and more intimate relationships, especially those we share with our partners, hold the potential to become "I-Thou" relationships — more sacred, deeper. I-Thou reflects a relationship in which the "Thou" in question is linked to an Eternal Thou. These are relationships based on mutual curiosity and love. But when so much of our "best self" has been on display all day, we are sometimes left drained for the relationships that matter most. We are on autopilot at best, and we can become aggressive, withholding, mean-spirited, and selfish at worst. "My partner will understand," we feebly hope. "I don't really need to impress them."

It's usually around 6 p.m. when my less-than-best self appears. Its entrance generally coincides with Leon and me regrouping after a day at work. I have arranged my schedule so that I am with our children in the afternoons. Homework hour rolls into screen time. Screen time rolls into guitar practice. Car ride after car ride after car ride, shuttling three active children between their afternoon activities, brings us to dinnertime. Hence we reach the twenty-minute stretch wherein a variety of healthy foods (that the kids are reluctant to eat) and unhealthy foods (that they eat with gusto! Read: Doritos!) are consumed.

And then my husband walks in. He has returned to a refuge from the world of work, with all of its inspired and less inspired

---

1. Martin Buber, *I and Thou* (London: Bloomsbury, 2013), 3–4.

aspects. For him, home is a place where he can be held, seen, and known. It is also a place to rest. The concept of rest is usually the furthest thing from my mind when I am at home. I see our home as an extension of my work. There are more clothes to fold or sibling squabbles to break up. Thus, by 6:10 p.m., friction inevitably mounts between my husband and me. Now that he has arrived, I turn to him to pull his weight as "staff" on the home front; he just wants to have dinner. My frustration ("Can you please run the bath?") is met with his critique ("Do you really think Doritos is a healthy choice?"). You can see how these quips about minor issues can quickly kindle a negative atmosphere at home.

As Aryeh Ben David has aptly written, every interaction creates a vibration, like plucking strings on a guitar.[2] When two string instruments are placed in a room and a string is plucked on one of the instruments, that same string will vibrate on the other instrument. Likewise, when my string is plucked, the strings around me will vibrate and pick up the same sound. The sounds and tones we bring into our partnerships reverberate. A neutral, angry, or kind tone from us will be matched by a neutral, angry, or kind tone in our partners. Our first step, as with all reflective work with our partners, is to check in with ourselves and ask, *Ayeka?*

---

2. Aryeh Ben David, *Becoming a Soulful Educator* (Woodstock, VT: Jewish Lights, 2011), 13–14.

🍃 *Where am I in my current relationship? What do I appreciate and love about my partner?*

🍃 *What drives me crazy about them? How do I contribute to dynamics of closeness or distance, adventure or boredom in my relationship? Do I crave or long for more?*

🍃 *If I were to imagine my relationship as more loving or connected, what would it look like? What's holding me back from moving in that direction?*

🍃 *What is one piece of advice I can give myself to help me move in that direction?*

As we know from earlier Ayeka exercises, change is not grand and sweeping with an applauding audience; change happens incrementally. It happens when we stay connected even though we feel like hiding. It happens when we put down the phone as our partner walks into the room so that we can give her/him our full attention. It comes in the fifteen uninterrupted minutes of sipping tea on the couch at the end of the day or in the thirty-minute shared walk outside — phones buried deep in pockets.

Meant to Be

Sometimes it takes a fresh set of eyes to offer perspective. One Shabbat afternoon last summer, after bickering about some topic that has since faded into unimportance, Leon and I found ourselves gravitating toward singing the same *zemirot* (songs) traditionally sung on Shabbat late afternoons. He was in the kitchen and I was at the table finishing my tea. We were both in our separate worlds, doing our own thing. I was savoring the few quiet moments at the end of a busy day hosting friends and colleagues for lunch, with many children playing, squabbling, and stealing cookies. He was tidying up so that the mountain of dishes in the sink, from the afternoon of entertaining, wouldn't bury us alive once Shabbat was over. While we were alone in our own thoughts, we found ourselves singing together. Our voices grew in strength, complexity, and harmony as we finished our song. My sister, who had been staying with us for a few weeks and was witness to our spontaneous duet, smiled in our direction. "The two of you were meant to be together," she said.

The idea of *bashert* (meant to be) isn't only a concept that belongs to matchmakers from the shtetl. It's a concept that dates back to rabbinic times. "Forty days before the formation of an embryo, a heavenly voice issues forth and proclaims, 'The daughter of so-and-so for so-and-so; this particular house for so-and-so; this particular field for so-and-so'" (Sotah 2a). If only the channels to heavenly communication were opened in my twenties and I had known I would meet Leon ten years later in pre-monsoon weather of Mumbai, India, I would have saved myself a lot of anguish and many hours of eating mediocre desserts on blind dates.

For those of you who have a hard time believing in the concept of *bashert*, or "destined" for a particular person (my sometimes-cynical self included): I actually believe that many different people hold the potential of being "right" for each of us. After all, isn't it hard work and active commitment that make long-term relationships work? But I think that the combination of our labor (nobody met their *bashert* while sitting under a rock) and a good dose of divine spirit creates the readiness for two people to come together and build a life. When that happens, something miraculous is at play.

Perhaps putting our faith in *bashert* helps us understand that there is something greater than the two of us. There is a reason for our meeting; there is something great that only the combination of the two of us can bring to the world. While the miracle may be a one-time occurrence, making good on our *bashert* is the unfolding work of our lives.

When we summon our imaginative powers to believe in the concept of *bashert*, we are also essentially endorsing the notion that our coupledom is more than just the two of us. In Jewish spiritual terms, this idea is called *kedushat habayit* (the sanctity of the home). When a couple first marries, the notion of joint purpose is intuitive. Wedding speeches, toasts at the reception, and promises made under a wedding canopy all conspire toward this lofty goal.

But as the years stretch on and challenges accumulate, these hopes might melt away or lose some of their power. Interests change. Domestic roles may become fixed. Inevitable family crises can bring two people closer together or drive a wedge between them. The intensity, passion, and focused "oneness" that characterized the earlier years of the marriage fade. In Jewish texts, the impulse for union is described poetically: "A man will leave his father and his mother, and will cleave to his wife, and they will become one flesh" (Genesis 2:24). This condition of *basar echad*, or "one flesh," is explained by S'forno, the Italian medieval biblical commentator: "They are to work together in such close union as if there were in fact only one of them."[3]

Creating a Joint Project

For my husband and me, *kedushat habayit* was reflected in our shared work with a small Jewish community on the East End of Long Island several years after we married. We approached the task with the vigor of start-up entrepreneurs.

But first, some background.

I had left for Israel right after graduating college. There I had built a life — work, community, friends, and an emerging (and more observant) spiritual life — in Jerusalem. I met Leon in India; and a year later, I followed him back to New York. He was more professionally established in New York, where he had founded a center for Jewish studies; I had more flexibility.

Soon after landing on the Upper West Side, I walked into L'Occitane in search of cream that rivaled the Dead Sea–based Ahava products I had been using. When the clerk asked if I wanted to join their "community," my heart leapt. I was in search of like-minded souls who could share and strengthen my vision of the world — as I had in Israel and part of why leaving there felt so wrenching. Little did I know that she was simply asking me to join their mailing list! Happily, my community-building savvy led me to develop a real community of like-minded young Jewish professionals in New York, one which I knew would be hard to leave.

In the book of our lives, I would title the chapter about our years in Manhattan as "Separate Together." Leon, very

---

3. S'forno commentary on Genesis 2:24, *basar echad*.

dedicated to his work, would dress in the uniform of an Upper East Side mercenary: jacket, tie, and button-down shirt. He would head out at 8:30 a.m. and return home just shy of the 9 p.m. evening news — a standard "day at the office" for a rising Jewish professional and rabbi-turned-educator whose congregation comprised adult students eager to engage with Jewish tradition and culture.

I, on the other hand, would go from bed to my home office, a desk set up in our kitchen. There I plugged away at independent consulting jobs and an emerging small business counseling marrying couples. Our togetherness took the form of sushi dinners and Saturday-morning coffee in bed with the *New York Times* and a big decision in front of us: Which synagogue were we in the mood for — spiritual or the one nearby?

When Leon suggested we move to the East End of Long Island, I am sure the ambivalent look on my face matched the mixed feelings I felt inside. "I think we should go," he said.

I met his surety with disbelief. Now — only a few short years into building a life in New York after moving from Israel? How could I possibly move again? I was settling into my new life in Manhattan. The pace, the planning, the grit: I had finally learned how to keep up with my New York life. This took some serious adjusting from my prior base, Jerusalem, where time is measured by the days until the next Sabbath (and wishing your cab driver "Shabbat Shalom" on Wednesday is not considered strange).

"I need a change, a new challenge," said my husband of three years. He looked at me with warm eyes. His grounded and methodical nature is often the opposite life force (*ezer k'negdo*) to my whimsical and impetuous one.

"I don't make so many wrong decisions," he said. "Can you trust me?"

We held a farewell picnic before we set out on our next journey. Sag Harbor, New York, is a small village that seasonally becomes a summer playground for wealthy New Yorkers. The year-round population simmers at around two thousand, boiling over to about six thousand in the summer months.

"You are now the team," our friend Elana told us. "In the city, everything can distract you. When you are out there, you will just have yourselves to rely on."

We took her blessing as our challenge. Could we become the team? As parents, we had practice as teammates. Together we were raising Tamir, then two years old. Could that effort extend to building a Jewish community?

In our roles as rabbi and Jewish educator of Sag Harbor, our shared passion motivated us. Our small wooden home at the top of Liberty Street became a laboratory that incubated ideas for new programs and new strategies for outreach. When a congregant lingered long after kiddush on Friday night, we knew that an invitation for Shabbat dinner would be most welcomed. When a congregant whom we invited for Passover Seder also wanted to bring her extended family, our ready answer was "With pleasure!" Our role was to bring the gift of Jewish home and hospitality to this yoga-loving, kale-eating community.

Not only could we do it but taking up the challenge of this "extended team-building exercise" turned out to be one of the best decisions of our married life.

While not all couples work together professionally, commitment to a joint project that extends beyond caring for your kids and home can take many forms. For some couples, it's a shared interest — a love of animals, pickling, or politics. For others, it's a shared outlook — charitable giving, healthy living, hosting events for family and friends. These interests and outlooks may be the ones that drew you together. Investing more in these activities will energize your relationship and model for your children commitment to something greater than the four walls of your home.

Ayeka Workbook

)) *What is your sense of purpose as a couple?*

)) *What is something that only the two of you can do together?*

)) *How do you want to grow (and nurture) your sense of joint purpose?*

)) *Which obstacles get in your way?*

)) *What is a small step you can take toward cultivating your joint purpose?*

The Shadow Side of a Joint Project

A strong sense of mission comes with a shadow side. Standing side by side while facing a common purpose can erode intimacy between couples. We were sometimes so focused on facing outward, toward our community, that we forgot to face each other — to reinforce and revive the bonds between us. The wisdom of *kedushat habayit* is in remembering the importance of pivoting: outward toward the common cause, then inward toward each other.

I felt this most acutely about a decade later when we moved to Israel. We were thick into our new joint project — becoming Israeli. Leon and I were each pursuing purposeful careers and raising Israeli children together. We are both very competent codirectors of Berkowitz & Morris LTD, but we found ourselves heads of very separate departments. And although our household runs efficiently, we discovered that the thinning of our joint purpose can present risks of a different sort.

Like when I blurted out, "I don't feel like you are interested in what is going on in my life." Ten-thirty at night is never a good time to begin these kinds of conversations, but for some reason, I couldn't help myself.

This was after several nights of Leon coming home late. We had been completing the requisite check-ins: "Are you good? Still alive?" "Good." "Are you also good? Still alive?" "Good." The rabbis of the Talmud understood the risk of couples growing apart when their focus is divided. The phrase *basar echad* (being one flesh) connotes more than sexual intimacy. It leads us to think about a single shared purpose. The reality, as the Talmud suggests, may fall short. In a story from Ketubot 62b, the rabbis relay a story of Rav Rehumi:

> Rav Rehumi, who was studying in [the school] of Raba at Mahoza, used to return home [once a year] on the eve of every Day of Atonement (Yom Kippur). On one occasion, he was so drawn in by his studies [that he forgot to return home]. His wife was expecting [him every moment, saying,] "He is coming soon, he is coming soon." As he did not arrive, she became so depressed that tears began to flow from her eyes. He was [at that moment] sitting on a roof. The roof collapsed under him and he was killed.

The wife's dashed hope is poignantly and beautifully communicated by the literary device of repetition: "He is coming soon, he is coming soon." After relating the story, the rabbis give us their takeaway: "This teaches how much one must be careful [in not causing pain to one's spouse], as [Rav Rehumi] was punished severely for causing anguish to his wife, even inadvertently."

Rav Rehumi and his wife are typologies, not roles assigned by gender or occupation. Much is at stake, warn the rabbis, when we become so exclusively focused on our own work and our own lives that we forget about the person on the other side, waiting for us to arrive at home.

Ayeka Workbook

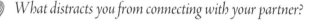

- What distracts you from connecting with your partner?
- Identify one distraction in particular. What is one way you might quiet the distraction or preoccupation?

Sometimes when I ask *Ayeka?* I am afraid of the answer. I try to place myself in a position of being ready to embrace whatever might emerge. Autopilot is the safer mode: you keep moving forward, no questions asked. But your vitality, and the vitality of your relationship, may suffer. While it's hard to do, creating a regular practice of asking *Ayeka?* can become our spiritual anchor.

4

Differences in
Parenting Styles
A Spur to Growth

Long before having children, I loved delving into Leon's world. He is from a small town in Pennsylvania, and I am from a suburb of Boston. He was the only Jewish kid in his class; I grew up in a place where all schools (not only private schools) were closed on Yom Kippur. Of course, we have much in common — our love of coffee, our passion for travel, and our love for all things Indian. Then there are the big things that really led us into each other's arms — feeling understood by the other, our shared sense of humor, and deep personal connection. But in our early years of marriage, what I found most fascinating was all the ways in which we took in the world *differently*.

Take how we each manage time, for instance. Leon is never late for anything, or at least not if he can help it. I, on the other hand (some of you will cringe when you read this!) — if I am finding parking *at the time* a meeting starts, I congratulate myself for being *on time*. My operating principle is that it takes ten minutes to get anywhere. Turns out, it usually takes longer.

Leon also has a different approach to life than I do. Everything he does is procedural, incremental. Before a trip, he starts to set aside his packing items on a shelf a week in advance. The process of packing gets done, no drama, no nonsense. For me, it's an "all or nothing" experience. Everyone needs to clear out of my way as I devote a good two hours to get into the "packing zone," laying out all of my clothes and accessories on my bed before I begin. I like to block out my time. I like to delve into a topic, task, or idea. Leon, on the other hand, enjoys multitasking and quickly moving from task to task, topic to topic.

When we were first getting to know each other, I found it fascinating to be close to the inner workings of someone else who experienced the world differently. His style began to influence how I moved through the world. No longer was I chronically late for everything. I learned to leave the house five minutes earlier than planned and arrive a bit *closer* to "on time."

I found that our particular ways reflected the worlds we came from. The long perspective he brought to his daily activities was the expression of years of accumulated experience. There were so many more layers of *who he was* than each encounter revealed. And I wanted to uncover each one.

My way of moving through the world elevated his life too: my social ease, my adaptability, my ability to find the fun in most situations. He eagerly embraced my life story, learning about how my father's youthful vigor and sense of humor influenced my own. He saw how my mother's immigrant background enabled her to open up easily in new social contexts and become adaptive, which was a model for me growing up.

Our openness to discovery characterized the first years of our marriage.

But once we began planning our family, the differences between us — once appreciated as my yin to his yang, together more whole than each piece alone — turned into sharp points. Cautious by nature, Leon became overly concerned about the foods I ate while pregnant. His overreactions were frequently met with an exasperated "Oh, come on!" from yours truly. At the beach, my laissez-faire attitude toward safety kept me on my towel — watching our toddler run toward the waves — while Leon lept up to save him from impending doom. Our styles clashed, inviting confrontation and disgruntlement. I became less eager to peel back the layers of who he is. I became less curious, less interested in discovery, more interested in fortifying my own emerging identity as a young mother.

The old adage "opposites attract" may feel true when couples are first getting to know each other, but years into a relationship, the excitement of being opposites can fade and turn oppositional. When we engage with difference, conflict often arises, which can put everyone at home on edge. When we disengage with difference, we are often avoiding, shutting down, or surrendering to our partner so that we don't experience the uncomfortable feelings that conflict brings out in us.

Difference Brings Insight

The question isn't how to avoid conflict in our relationships. Conflict is part and parcel of being in a relationship. Conflict will inevitably arise, and when it does, we can either react by keeping it going or turning the dynamic into creative tension that can yield new insights.

The idea that conflict holds the potential for being productive is illustrated by the very *first* intimate relationship in the Bible: that of Adam and Eve. The second chapter of Genesis tells the story of Adam's creation. God creates the first man from the dust of the earth (the name Adam comes from the Hebrew word for earth, *adamah*). After placing Adam in the Garden of Eden, God realizes, "It is not good for a (hu)man being to be alone" (Genesis 2:18). God's first tactic to remedy Adam's loneliness is to bring the animals to Adam and have him name them. Adam names each animal as a way of asserting his influence over them. It isn't the ideal relationship to address Adam's loneliness, and God agrees: "But for Adam there was not found a *help-meet (ezer k'negdo)* for him" (Genesis 2:20).

In response, God creates Eve from Adam's rib/side: finally a fitting help meet for Adam.

What exactly is a help-meet? It's a strange word and its meaning is open to interpretation. We can begin by parsing the Hebrew term *ezer k'negdo*. *Ezer* means "help," and *k'negdo* means "against him." It is the kind of relationship that God envisions for Adam. Maybe it's also the kind of relationship we all need.

What kind of relationship can be both helpful and contrary at the same time? If you are going to help me, help! Don't go against me! I imagine how frustrating it would be if I were at the bottom of the stairs with a whole load of groceries that I needed to carry up to the third floor. How could being *against me* help at all? I want my partner to take a few bags, for heaven's sake!

But there are situations when *help*, coupled with *going against*, can bring more nuance and lead to deeper truth. Take an example from the professional world. While it's comfortable for a colleague to be a yes-person, it's more productive if their agreeable attitude is coupled with a different perspective. Better than saying "Yes! Let's move ahead with that project!" it's so much more helpful when a colleague says, "That project sounds like a wonderful idea, but there are a few considerations I think we should look into that can make it better."

The same goes for our intimate relationships. Rabbi Walter Wurzburger quotes Rav Joseph Ber Soloveitchik's interpretation that Eve was not simply to function as Adam's yes-woman; she was supposed to help him *by being against him* and offering an opposing perspective.

> The Rav [Rav Joseph Ber Soloveitchik] interpreted the verse that Eve was to function as Adam's *ezer k'negdo* in the sense that Eve was not simply to function as Adam's help-meet, but that she was supposed to help him — by being *k'negdo* — by offering opposing perspectives.[1]

Opposition *is* what is most helpful.

Though it would feel easier if Leon were to unconditionally support every idea, plan, or approach I have with our kids, in the big picture it is a lot more helpful when he can balance us with his angle of the picture. Here's an example.

It's the start of the school year and I am sharing the very intricate after-school plan I have envisioned for each child. Yael is a great swimmer, and her swim coach invited her to be on the swim team. I think that three hours of swimming every week is a bit too much, and I want her to explore more options and try new classes. She's only eight, after all.

Leon thinks differently. It's important for a kid to excel at something. Neither of us were "sporty" kids, but we saw from the side how confident sporty kids can be. Encouraging our daughter to seriously "take on" swimming, Leon claimed, could be a huge boost to her self-esteem.

There is no question that the difference of opinion slows down a process. (I just want to have their afternoon schedule lined up already!) But when we welcome the differences, a more nuanced insight can be uncovered.

---

1. "Rav Joseph B. Soloveitchik as Posek of Post-Modern Orthodoxy," *Tradition* 29 (1994): 17.

Ayeka Workbook

 When your partner offers an opposing perspective about a situation in your family, what is your first reaction?

 How do you imagine you would react differently if you could see the opposing perspective as "helpful" in deepening your understanding of yourself, your children, or the situation?

 What's one small step you can take to help you move in that direction?

While some of you might be nodding, "Well, of course, differences of opinion are good and important," the truth is, living with differences is not at all easy. There is so much noise preventing me from being open to the different approaches offered by my partner. There's tone and sarcasm: "Did you really think it was a good idea to leave the ice cream in the car while you were driving the kids around to their activities?" There are also competing priorities and values. While one of us, educationally minded, wants to limit screen time, the other prefers the kids take in more of Netflix's hypnosis, granting us a few rare moments of R & R.

If I worked on pausing and returning to the good intentions that I had when we first fell in love, I might be able to dial back some of the noise getting in the way. It might even bring me to say, "Hey, I love you, and let's understand that we come from different perspectives here. I want to understand you and your perspective better. I think it can really help our family."

Take the example above of the melted ice cream. Instead of becoming defensive or feeling hurt, I can appreciate how Leon hates wasting food. Instead of feeling dismissed, Leon can appreciate that I am balancing work and domestic life, which at times might involve leaving groceries in the car while running our kids around to their activities.

Ayeka Workbook

 Think of a situation when it was challenging for you to appreciate the different approach your partner offered.

 What about the situation was challenging? Think about what was at the core of the challenge.

Name one value, perspective, or attitude you can appreciate about your partner from that place.

When I have facilitated our Becoming a Soulful Parent sessions, I have often found the session on appreciating the difference in parenting styles to be one of the most challenging. A common dynamic is that one parent sees him- or herself as the "main parent" and the other as the assistant. The assumed primacy of one parent's approach can become the unwritten rule.

Another common pitfall is the presumption that there is an objective "right" and "wrong" answer. I remember in one session, a father expressed deep concern that his wife allowed their son to ride his bike without a helmet. How could appreciating her lackadaisical attitude toward safety be a good thing?

With my children, I strive to deflect when I don't like their behavior: "It's not them, it's the behavior." I should strive to do the same with my partner. For instance, in the scenario above, the father's instinct was "Can you believe how negligent my wife is!" But he could reframe his approach: "She moves through the world with a lot more trust than I do." This puts him in a more appreciative place from which it is less vitriolic to discuss expectations around safety at home.

Part of connecting to our soul voice is also knowing intuitively when difference turns dangerous. When we feel unsafe, unappreciated, or unloved, we need to know when to ask for help to remedy the dynamics. Contention isn't always generative. When a relationship no longer feels life-giving on a regular basis, and when bouncing back no longer seems possible, it may be time for a therapist, marriage counselor, or social worker to step in.

Bless the Difference

Like so much of our striving to become soulful parents, it all comes back to recognizing and honoring our unique God-given soul — and our partner's God-given soul too. Your partner is different from you, holding different opinions, values, and attitudes from you. It's all by design.

Honoring difference is hard spiritual work. It has implications far beyond the intimate walls of our homes. Religious and ethnic groups can become locked in battle when they refuse to recognize difference. As Rabbi Jonathan Sacks writes, "The test of faith is whether I can make space for difference.

Can I recognize God's image in someone who is not in my image, whose language, faith, ideals are different from mine? If I cannot, then I have made God in my image instead of allowing him to remake me in his."[2] Since we are all in God's image, we each reflect an aspect of the Divine. We all hold a portion of the truth; none of us holds all of it.

When I don't allow space for the different worldview and attitude that my partner brings to our family, I am denying that he, too, reflects God's image.

Appreciating my partner's differences also teaches our kids that there is more than one way to do things in life. We're commonly told that parents should always be on the same page so that our children receive clear, consistent messages. But when our kids see that their parents are able to appreciate difference in the other, it may help them learn how to embrace difference and be resilient in their own future relationships.

It takes work — spiritual work — to declutter the messy space where the dust of difference settles. Aggressive speech, criticism, or shutting down may be our instinctual responses. By contrast, getting curious is our spiritual one. It requires us to turn down our ego voices, which are usually shouting, "My way is the best!"

So the next time your partner takes a different tack with your children, make room for it. If you can, bless the difference.

---

2. Jonathan Sacks, *The Dignity of Difference: Avoiding the Clash of Civilizations* (London: Continuum, 2004), 201.

5

Rivalry, Competition, and Comparison

Lessons Only a Sibling Can Teach

When I was younger, I worshipped my sister. She had the most eclectic clothes and I wanted to wear them. She had the best music cassettes (Wham!, Hall & Oats) and I wanted to listen to them. She played the most creative drama games (like the time we played "classroom" and she was the teacher who charged me for the school supplies she sourced from the kitchen drawer) and I thought she was so clever. With three years' difference between us, I couldn't wait for the day we would finally be in the same high school together. I was a rising freshman and she was a graduating senior. She wasn't particularly popular (back then, eclectic kids never were) but she was original, older, and a member of *my family*. Being with her outside of our home was like a secret bond revealed under the fluorescent lights of our high school's gray locker–lined hallway. When I would see her standing around with her friends, my heart leapt. Sometimes I would overdo it and ask her for a hug. She would shrug and turn back to her friends, ambivalent about revealing her close relationship with her younger sister in public.

While we got along a lot of the time, we also *really* knew how to fight. I was particularly skilled at driving her crazy. I could upend her status as the older sister in a way that would make Machiavelli proud. One time, I remember standing in front of her, and while I don't remember the content of the argument, I remember my response. She was getting worked up about something while I stood there calmly (of course *I* was calm, as *I* am the one recalling the story) and responded, "You don't need to yell at me. I can hear you. I am standing one foot away from you." My snarkiness only further escalated her rage and the pitch of her shouting pierced the heavens.

I aggravated her so much because, deep down, I was jealous. Whatever she had, I wanted it too. She had a boyfriend on a summer trip to Israel; what about me? She got to stay up an hour later than me on Saturday nights to watch *The Love Boat*; what was I, chopped liver? She had special time with our mom every Friday; did our mom love *her more?*

I didn't know how to value what *I wanted*; I just wanted what she had. She set a standard for me to follow. The world of possibility was only as big as the life she lived.

Siblings are our measuring sticks for what is possible. When the oldest is good at math, the younger sibling wonders why long division is hard for them. When the younger one has a lot of friends, the older one wonders why they have the same friend over every day.

The sibling relationship is a foundational building block of all of our social connections, and our homes are the living laboratory where experiments in this dynamic relationship play out.

"Children are hardwired for struggle," says Brené Brown.[1] She should know! She is a well-known author, researcher, and public speaker whose TED Talks and books on vulnerability, shame, courage, and empathy have become highly popular in mainstream culture.

Developing any new skill is a struggle, whether it's crawling, walking, writing, or learning numbers. We adults — having already developed core skills — struggle less than we did as children. We have built mechanisms to cope with familiar challenges: "Why drive a new way to work? It's much safer to go the way we always do." "Why try a new recipe? I will make the tried-and-true one, as I know it always turns out great." We learn that struggle is an uncomfortable feeling, and instinctively we learn how to minimize it.

Yet in our interpersonal relationships, we struggle. We feel competitive toward a coworker who gets more attention than we do at work, or jealous of a friend who seems to have it all together where we *clearly* do not. We want to stand out and get recognition but we get overlooked. Better understanding our own competitive feelings will give us a good measure of empathy when responding to sibling dynamics between our kids. For those of us with one child at home, they too will struggle as they notice the areas in which, in their eyes, they don't "measure up" to their friends.

So before we turn to our children, let's ask ourselves, *Ayeka?* Where are we in our feelings of competition toward others?

---

1. Brené Brown, "The Power of Vulnerability," TEDxHouston, October 6, 2010, https://www.ted.com/talks/brene_brown_on_vulnerability /transcript?language=en.

Ayeka Workbook

 On a scale of 1 to 10, where are you in comparing yourself to others?

 Imagine what your life might look like if you compared yourself to others less.

 Think back to chapter 2 where you reflected on your soul as a parent. What's a gift that you have that is uniquely you?

 What's a small step you can take to honor your unique gift?

Our ability to understand where we are regarding feeling competitive will help us maintain our connection to, and empathy for, our children, even when their bickering drives us crazy.

The Tragic Nature of Sibling Rivalry

Ernest Becker, author of *The Denial of Death*, moves sibling rivalry out of the private domain of the home, postulating that this dynamic signifies the tragic part of the human condition. He says that, contrary to popular belief, sibling rivalry is not related to kids being spoiled or selfish. Becker's theory is that these interactions express "the heart of the creature: the desire to stand out, to be the one in creation."[2]

---

2. Ernest Becker, *The Denial of Death* (New York: Free Press, 1973), 3–4.

This is the reason for the daily and usually excruciating struggle
with siblings: the child cannot allow himself to be second-best
or devalued, much less left out: "You gave him the biggest piece
of candy!" "You gave him more juice!" "Here's a little more, then."
"Now she's got more juice than me!" Sibling rivalry is a critical
problem that reflects the basic human condition: it is not that
children are vicious, selfish, or domineering. It is that they so
openly express man's tragic destiny: he must desperately justify
himself as an object of primary value in the universe; he must
stand out, be a hero, make the biggest possible contribution to
world life, show that he counts more than anything or anyone else.[3]

The reason siblings fight is not because they really *want*
more juice; they fight because getting less juice represents
being less. According to Becker, the spark that ignites conflict
with a sibling is the same one that gives them drive. It's their
ego voice clamoring for attention. Ego is good. But it is also
voracious and hard to satisfy, especially in children, whose
sense of themselves (their ego) is getting stronger day by day.

How do we address sibling rivalry? One way is to *move
beyond* the realm of our ego voice and the story it tells us while
moving into our soul voice and amplifying *its* story. When we
tap into our spiritual imagination, we can learn something
from how God creates the first human being, Adam. God gives
Adam a *neshamah*; in Hebrew, the root of the word *neshamah*
is *nun-shin-mem*, the same three-letter root that forms the
word for breath. By *breathing* into Adam's nostrils, God gives
him a soul and brings him to life. Adam is transformed from
an amalgam of flesh and bones into a living being. If we take
this idea to its logical conclusion, our soul — or that which
makes each one of us simply who we are — is also *what keeps*

---

3. Becker, *Denial of Death*, 3–4.

us alive. When we forget our *soul* by comparing ourselves to others, we die a small death.

The first sibling relationship in the Bible reflects this tragic reality.

In Genesis, the world's first parents, Adam and Eve, are expelled from the Garden of Eden and have two children: first Cain, then Abel. From the outset, the two are very different. Abel is a shepherd; Cain is a farmer. Early in their lives, they each bring an offering to God. Abel brings the best of his flock, while Cain brings fruit from his harvest. God accepts Abel's gift but rejects Cain's offering. In turn, Cain becomes downcast.

God speaks directly to Cain, asking, "Why are you distressed, and why has your face fallen?" There is no pause here for Cain to respond and say, "I am jealous of my brother, because his gift to You was accepted and mine was not!" God continues to offer Cain a degree of tough love: "Surely, if you do right, [you will be uplifted]." Some interpret this to mean, if you had brought the *best* of your fruits the way that Abel brought the best of his flock, you would not be so down. Finally, God warns, "But if you do not do right, sin crouches at the door; its urge is toward you." The consequence of Cain *not* doing his best will leave him vulnerable to the force of sin. However, God expresses continued belief in Cain: "Yet you can master it" (Genesis 4:6–7). That is, Cain has the potential to keep his jealous feelings toward his brother at bay.

The story doesn't end well. Cain buckles under the feeling that he is unworthy compared to his brother, and he ultimately kills Abel. God's prophecy comes true; sin, indeed, crouched at the door of Cain's jealousy.

Although Cain is upset because God seemingly does not value him — *compared to* how much God values Abel — God is communicating a different message. *Live up to* your *potential, Cain; this is not about your brother.*

This story's lesson for us, as parents, is clear. How can we build up our children's good qualities and encourage them to bring their best, especially in their sibling relationships?

Once we understand that our children compare themselves to one another, vying for our affirmation — and that this perception is at the core of sibling rivalry — we are guided to react with renewed perspective.

How can we see each of our kids as infinitely valuable, without comparing each to the other? How can the way *we* see them become a model for how they see themselves? We want them to be able to say to themselves, "So what if my brother is good at math. That doesn't impact me! I am me! I am great with animals. My worth isn't tied to the fact that my brother is better at math than I am! And, in fact, it's great that he is *him* and he is good at math. Cool!" I am not sure my young daughter is really capable of saying that, but that's how I want her to feel internally.

Ayeka
Workbook

 Name three unique and precious qualities about each of your children. Write them down.

 Remind them of these traits that you appreciate about them throughout the day and even while cooling down after a sibling brawl.

My go-to place when my kids are not getting along with one another is to threaten *big* consequences.

I yell. I demand. I say things like, "Now listen here, that will be enough of this behavior, you hear me?! There will be *big* consequences!" When I react quickly, I don't pause to ask, *Ayeka?*

Where am I?

What is being triggered in me that I am reacting so strongly?

Maybe I am embarrassed that they are acting this way?

Maybe they are ruining the "ideal family" picture I have in my head?

But it would be good for me to remember that their fighting has nothing to do with me. It's about them working out their own relationship. Once I can get clear about that, I can open up space within myself to listen.

Once, the dynamics between Tamir and Yael were heating up all Shabbat. I called a meeting. "We are going to be in one another's lives forever. You will always be siblings to each other, we will always be your parents. Now let's make the most of it," I declared.

My husband had his own declaration: "I want peace in our home — *shalom bayit.*"

Though our pronouncements reflect our family's ultimate values, they can only go so far. Without creating space to listen to our kids' underlying needs at that moment, the value pronouncements remain slogans — easy to repeat and easier to dismiss.

I asked my kids to tell me what was really going on behind the scenes and slowly, amazingly, the energy shifted. They moved away from the defensive "He's so dumb" and "She's always annoying me" to what was at the core.

My son said, "I never get any attention. She always gets all the attention. I am the one who is always left out." After sharing this, he buried himself beneath couch pillows to insulate himself from what was to follow.

My daughter responded, "I always say nice things about Tamir and he never says nice things about me. Why doesn't he ever say nice things about me?"

The ironclad defenses were slowly melting away. My daughter wanted her brother to think highly of her. My son wanted more attention from us.

In other words, "annoying us" is not their motivation to fight with each other. They are fighting because they have a human need that is trying to be expressed.[4]

Harnessing the Power of Siblings

My favorite "consequence" for my children not getting along has to do with harnessing their power (so evident as they spar!) for good. It can be any kind of joint effort. The dynamic often shifts when they depend on one another.

The other day, Tamir woke up in the morning eager to present a highly intricate card trick before the eager eyes of Yael and Shalva. When one of them figured out the trick — "You flipped over both of the cards instead of just the top one!" — my son became upset: "Why do you always mess up everything!" The dynamic escalated until they left for school. With their backpacks slung over their shoulders, they slouched out the door, turning and mimicking my cheerful "Have a good day!" with a heavy dose of sarcasm. After their morning skirmish, "good" and "day" weren't really words that went together well.

---

4. This idea is based on the theory of nonviolent communication expressed by Inbal Kashtan in "Parenting with Nonviolent Communication (NVC)," YouTube, April 2, 2007, 8:15, https://www.youtube.com/watch?v=IQO7h9MNCqI.

A few moments before they left, I told them there would be no playdates that afternoon. Instead, there were three tasks that they would need to complete — together.

When they got home later that day, I presented them with my list: take out the recycling, prepare their little sister's "birthday chair" (with balloons and signs), and empty the dishwasher. They could choose the order. When my son suggested "Let's split up the list," I firmly reminded him of the rules. They had to do it together. With recycling in hand, they ran down the stairs (no doubt betting who could get downstairs the fastest).

The time between the fight in the morning and the afternoon détente was critical for shifting their dynamic. So much had happened in their lives between the card trick and 2:30 p.m. Distance was put "between the match and the matchbox,"[5] preventing another flare-up. Their energy can spark a fire or, when creatively redirected, can help me get a lot of chores done in the house! I heard them laugh together as they returned from their chores. They managed to accomplish only two out of the three tasks I set for them. I didn't mind.

My concerns about my children's relationships mellow when I consider how my sister and I relate to each other now that we are adults. I prize my relationship with my sister as one of the most important in my life. Even though we live thousands of miles apart from each other (with the Atlantic between us), we are partners in caring for our aging parents and we prioritize visiting each other in the summertime. As Baz Luhrmann wryly declares in his song "Everybody's Free (to Wear Sunscreen)": "Be nice to your siblings. They are the best link to your past,

---

5. Alan Morinis, *Everyday Holiness* (Boston: Trumpeter Books, 2007), 58–59.

and the people most likely to stick with you in the future."[6]

My children certainly still joust and annoy and aggravate one another. As my son hurls at my daughter in the background, "You sound like a dying cow when you sing!" I sit at the kitchen table, both hands wrapped around my mug of mint tea, its steam warming my face and soothing the worry lines on my forehead. Though I can't change their dynamics, I *can* offer key interventions, change my perspective, and know that they are learning lessons only they can teach one another.

6. Baz Luhrmann, vocalist, "Everybody's Free (to Wear Sunscreen)," by Mary Schmich, Nigel Swanston, and Tim Cox, on *Something for Everybody*, EMI, 1997.

6

Home Layout and Family Routine
Opening a Door to the Divine

My son rearranges his room about once a month. Behind the closed door, we hear him moving his bed from one end of the room to the other, or his synthesizer to *this* wall instead of *that* one. By the end of the process, there's always a pile of discarded items outside his door. I sift through the debris from his monthly ritual, usually salvaging only the pictures from his early elementary school days.

When I ask him why he engages in this exercise, he responds, "It's boring when my room stays the same. I feel more creative when I can change things around."

Wow!

And then I think back to how I was as a child. When I changed the location of my pillow, moving it from the head of my bed to the foot, it was groundbreaking. "New perspective! A whole new world!" I could now look at the poster of my favorite teen idol and gaze into his eyes as I drifted off to sleep. My room was my kingdom. Any slight shift of a chair or bed would create a new flow and new possibilities.

There is something elemental about space. The space we live in, and all of our stuff, is not just a conglomeration of objects, clothes, books, and furniture we bump into. Instead, our homes contain and express our lives. How we organize and arrange this nook, that chair, and those cups creates the internal blueprint for the place we construct and reconstruct with each new stage.

For me, it all started with the drinking cups.

Once upon a time, whenever my kids were thirsty, they would ask me for a glass of water. Though I was glad they were staying hydrated, I would feel put out each time they interrupted me for a glass. Of course, they had no choice, as the glasses were kept in the cupboard above the sink, which is out of reach when you are four feet tall. I moved the cups to the lower shelf near the fridge and voilà! Independence! Self-sufficiency!

In our Becoming a Soulful Parent group, one mother mentioned how she wanted her family to hang out more in the family room together. Until that point, her kids spent hours in the playroom, whose major attraction was the LEGO table. Now that she's moved the LEGO table into the living room, the table works like a magnet, drawing her kids there.

Another father lamented that his library on British politics is stored away and replaced by a slew of parenting how-to books. He reasoned that this is probably as good as it gets at this stage in their life. Their bookshelf is now piled high with other accoutrements — wipes, teething rings, and children's books (especially since they have twins!). In an effort to honor what was important to him, he and his wife set to rearranging their bookshelf, with his British politics tomes now front and center. Now he even reads from them sometimes *to* the babies as a way of lulling them to sleep.

Name a value that you hold important for your home (examples: more family time, developing a child's independence, intellectual stimulation, welcoming guests, time as a couple).

If you could change one thing about the physical arrangement of your home to encourage that value more, what would you change?

What is one small step you can take toward making that change?

The Spirituality of Our Physical Spaces

Books about home organization encourage us to sort through one room at a time, setting up our homes the way kindergarten classrooms are organized: every item has its place.[1] I like this approach because everyone in the family knows exactly where each item belongs and how to return it to its spot at the end of the day. (If only life was as well run as an early childhood center!) Lately, however, a different perspective on home organization has been drawing my attention.

---

1. Julie Morgenstern, *Organizing from the Inside Out*, 2nd ed. (New York: Henry Holt, 2004), 59–66.

Marie Kondo,[2] Japanese "tidying" guru, sits in a prayerful position and offers a meditation before tidying someone else's home. She sets an intention about how the home can express the family's hopes and dreams. Together, she and her client set out to do the hard work of sorting, filing, and discarding items by category. With her unconventional approach, she helps people bring more harmony, flow, and even joy to an otherwise tedious household chore.[3]

What strikes me most is how spiritual Marie Kondo and her methods are. She has tapped into, and made accessible, an ancient concept held by so many faiths and cultures: our physical home can be the place where something *beyond* physical "stuff" can dwell. The Chinese spiritual philosophy known as feng shui might call this something "good energy" or "invisible forces." In Jewish tradition, we speak of the *Shekinah*, the female aspect of the Divine — literally translated as "the One Who Dwells."

The *Shekinah* is said to dwell just above the spiritual *house* of the Jewish people (Shemot Rabbah 2:2) — the *Beit ha-Mikdash* (the Temple) in Jerusalem.[4] To fuel our spiritual batteries, we were once encouraged to *go out* on a physical pilgrimage to the Temple, our national home. But once this "big house" was destroyed, the rabbis of the Talmud did something interesting.

---

2. Marie Kondo is the author of *The Life-Changing Magic of Tidying Up* (Berkeley, CA: Ten Speed Press, 2014) and host of the successful Netflix series *Tidying Up with Marie Kondo*.

3. KonMari Media, Inc., "About," konmari.com, accessed May 12, 2020, https://konmari.com/pages/about.

4. Even though this home was destroyed in 70 CE, its western retaining wall is still visited as a point of pilgrimage for Jewish people the world over.

They declared that every Jewish synagogue or house of study was a *mikdash me'at* (small sanctuary), a virtual stand-in for the Temple as the center of our lives (Megillah 29a). In this way, they shifted the spiritual imagination of the Jewish people *inward*, encouraging us to tap into the holy energy filling our own (small) spaces.

What would it mean for us to imagine our homes as places where the Divine could dwell? (Just a friendly reminder here: let's not let language limit our imaginations. The Divine can be God, a sense of harmony, or the recognition of moments that feel holy, to name a few interpretations.)

Ayeka Workbook

⟫ *Have you ever experienced a moment in your home as sacred or holy (however you might define that)?*

⟫ *If you wanted to experience more of these moments, what would need to be cleared away?*

⟫ *What is one small step you can take in that direction?*

I am the first to admit that it is hard for me to experience my home life as relaxing, let alone a sanctuary where the divine spirit can dwell. My home office is also the "mudroom," so school bags, coats, and unmatched gloves are all hanging out with me as I type away at my computer. My living room is piled with laundry. (I am working on teaching my kids that just because an item of clothing touched their body does not mean that it needs to be laundered!) Ingredients that will (magically) turn into dinner later are sprawled over the kitchen counter.

We experience several not-so-sacred moments in our home space, especially when I bring all the kids home from school at the same time. Bursting through the door, my children fling their respective backpacks hither and thither and then start negotiating who gets to watch my(!) computer first. "Homework first!" I shout to the air as I turn my attention to the dishes and the veggie plate that I busily prepare before they get to the pantry to snatch a snack. Coming home sometimes feels like starting a sprint, not relaxing into a sanctuary.

I'm always coming up with all sorts of new plans and approaches and charts of how things should be at home. But sometimes when I get home with the kids, I decide to do something different; I walk through the door and sit down.

Radical, right?

I happen to sit down on the comfiest chair in the house, the one that is situated right in the middle of the living room.

There I just relax for a few minutes.

Five to be exact. (My short-term life goal is to bring that number up to ten or even fifteen minutes, but five is a solid start.)

When I started to do this, I noticed something remarkable happen. My children, who would otherwise be running in all directions, slowed down. Like a balloon losing air, my youngest (the most energetic runner) gradually began to drift toward me, landing on my lap. The fact that I chose to experience our home as a place of rest and renewal, even if just for five minutes, invited her to do the same.

The idea of a divine presence dwelling in our homes can also invite us to be more expansive about the ways in which we celebrate time and elevate the day-to-day. In a sensitive literary interpretation of the passages in the Bible where the matriarch Sarah dies, the midrash helps us envision how our homes could be. In the story, a wife for Sarah's son Isaac is found soon after his mother's death.[5] The chapter ends with Isaac's marriage to Rebekah: "Isaac brought her into the tent of Sarah his mother. He took Rebekah as his, and she became his wife and he loved her. Then was Yitzchak comforted for the death of his mother" (Genesis 24:67).

A midrash fills in the gaps of the biblical story, answering the lurking question: What *exactly* did Isaac and Rebekah find in Sarah's tent that was so comforting? Was there something about the nature of the home space that Sarah built that can inspire us?

The midrash says:

Isaac brought her into the tent of his mother Sarah:

All the time Sarah was alive, there was a cloud fixed to the opening of her tent. When she died, the cloud disappeared. When Rebekah came, the cloud returned.

All the time Sarah was alive, the doors were open wide. When Sarah died, that generosity disappeared. When Rebekah came, the generosity returned.

All the time Sarah was alive, there was a blessing associated with the dough. When Sarah died, that blessing disappeared. When Rebekah came, it returned.

All the time Sarah was alive, there was a lamp lit from one Shabbat night to the next. When she died, that light disappeared. When Rebekah came, it returned. (Bereshit Rabbah 60:16)

---

5. Genesis 23:2: "Sarah died in Kiriath-arba — now Hebron — in the land of Canaan; and Abraham mourned Sarah and wept for her."

A cloud, an open door, dough, and light — four metaphors that can comfort and sustain us as we reimagine our home spaces. Each concept holds the potential to bring new insight in how we enter, plan, and celebrate our families in our homes.

The cloud (*anan*) at the opening of her tent, the first characteristic of Sarah's home, is resonant with the clouds of glory (*ananei hakavod*) that God sent to guide the Israelites as they wandered through the desert in the biblical account in the book of Numbers. The metaphor of the cloud can invite us to imagine the thresholds of our homes as significant. Instead of rushing into our homes, how might we gather ourselves before coming home? How might the traditional practice of touching a mezuzah or another ritual of entering become meaningful for us? Transitions into the home come in many shapes and sizes — a breath, a pause, a hope uttered for the energy you want to bring with you as you reconnect with your family.

The second characteristic of Sarah's home that set it apart was that her doors were opened expansively. Open doors invite in new guests and new friendships. Open doors challenge us to ask: How open are we to new ideas entering our home? How do we model responding to challenges beyond our comfort zone for our children? How open are we to the new ideas that our children bring into our home? Expansiveness connotes stretching the boundaries of what might sometimes feel comfortable. It might mean changing our plans sometimes when an urgent need arises — a neighbor who needs help, a news event that needs to be discussed.

The third characteristic is the "blessing in the dough." How can we elevate our experience around mealtime and breaking bread together? Few are the weekdays when my whole family gathers around the table for dinner. One night Tamir is at his camping club, another evening Yael has dance lessons and

Shalva is with a friend on a playdate. The magnetic draw of a kitchen table with food enjoyed equally by both kids and grown-ups holds open the potential for eating, reconnecting, and sharing news. Sometimes our dinnertime meals feel less than the blessed occasion I hope for. Aggravation and petty sibling fights get in the way of my kids being supportive and kind. Sometimes I see glimpses of blessing, such as the time when Yael gave Shalva advice about how to be a good friend, or another time when I got to share stories of my grandmother in India and how strangers were always welcome around her mother's table.

The final metaphor in the midrash about Sarah's home is about light. It's also the most mystical. When the light from candles in Sarah's tent lasts from one Shabbat and holiday celebration to the next, I imagine the power Sarah imbued in candlelight that made it worthy of lasting. When I think about it, the physical properties of a flame keep it pointing upward no matter how low it's held. Maybe the upward draw of flame reflects each person in the family. No matter what someone said or did to be disruptive or disrespectful, I can work from a baseline assumption that my son, daughters, husband, and I will never stay in that low place; we'll always be drawn upward. When I light candles on Friday night, the metaphor of an upward-searching flame is a powerful reminder to have faith that we are all capable of turning our warm light upward. That intention is something that I would like to bring with me to the next week.

Ayeka
Workbook

 Pick one of the metaphors from the midrash above. Which characteristic do you feel like you already incorporate into your home life?

Which concept would you want to bring into your home in concrete ways?

 What is one small step you can take toward manifesting that characteristic?

7

Chaos
An Opportunity for Insight

In the beginning God created the heavens and the earth. The earth was unformed and void, and darkness was upon the face of the deep; and the spirit of God hovered over the face of the waters. God said: "Let there be light." And there was light. God saw the light, that it was good; and God divided the light from the darkness. God called the light Day, and the darkness He called Night. There was evening and there was morning, one day. (Genesis 1:1–5)

Have you ever wondered why the Bible bothers to tell us about the initial chaotic state of the world? Why doesn't it just directly continue with "And then there was light" (*vayehi or*)? Life would be so much easier that way. So much more efficient. You begin, you create the container (heaven and earth), and then you focus on content. "Light! Insight! Keep it positive, people!"

But the Torah doesn't begin that way. Deeply embedded into the fabric of existence, from the very beginning of mythic time, is something called *tohu va'vohu*. "The earth was without form and void (*tohu va'vohu*)" (Genesis 1:1–2).

What is this mysterious *tohu va'vohu*? And why is it situated right at the beginning of time?

Tohu can be translated either as "chaos" or as "emptiness." It is an uncultivated state of being, untouched by the hand of order.

But then, as the second verse of Genesis relates, "The spirit of God hovered over the face of the waters." The chaotic state of the world is calmed and tamed by the *consciousness* that there is something that guides *tohu va'vohu* from above.

Maybe in all of the confusion, chaos, and nothingness there is a real "Something" that is whispering to us, calling to us, calming us. Some of us might call this Something "God." Some might call it a connection to something beyond ourselves, that which makes for good and brings harmony into the world. Finally, after the chaos comes order, God enters with a clear stage direction: "God said, 'Let there be light'; and there was light." From here, order proceeds straightforwardly:

God appreciates the light as "good."

God makes distinctions between light and darkness.

God names the light "day" and the darkness "night."

There was evening, there was morning: day one.

Sounds like any superhero — when met with a complex mess of impulses and life forces, God elegantly tames them into a manageable, efficient sequence of events.

Wouldn't it be nice if things followed such a clear sequence at home?

I declare, "Breakfast is ready!"

I say breakfast is tasty (everyone agrees).

Children stay at the table, eat breakfast, and clear their plates.

I call what they have done "admirable."

There was morning, there was breakfast: now we are off to school.

We might prefer the idea that order is always possible if we only work hard enough, or that our outer lives might radiate this sense of order and control. But our inner lives tell a different story.

Our inner lives are full of complexity, inconsistency, and sometimes a sense of confusion (even chaos). Our children might feel this way too. Instead of acknowledging confusion as a part of life, we are constantly trying to "do" something about it. We perpetuate the myth that if only we had the right plan, the right behavioral modification chart, the right "heart-to-heart talk" with our kids, our children will "get over" the *tohu va'vohu* they might feel inside.

Recognizing that *tohu va'vohu* is an essential stage in life can help us become less agitated when the clear structure of our lives is derailed. This knowledge can help us become less controlling as parents too.

But sometimes the realization that *tohu va'vohu* impacts us all fails to calm us. In those moments of insecurity and tumult, being open to believing that Something hovers above the chaos can offer a sense of comfort and strength.

Our children's development is also subject to *tohu va'vohu*. Understanding this helps give us perspective. Our children's development is not necessarily linear or direct. Their life experiences, like all of ours, oscillate between ups and downs. We experienced this recently with our son. Last year was a hard year for him. He didn't respect his teacher. He wasn't motivated to do his work. Angry outbursts were frequent. My heart sank, and I resigned myself, thinking, "I guess this is who he is now." This year we experienced a turnaround: a teacher he respects, a new close friend whom he loves, a goal of getting into a good middle school that motivates him to apply himself.

But recently his old attitudes resurfaced. He became impatient and obstinate. (Deep inhale.) I started to feel stress, wondering if everything that had been getting better was just an illusion.

Naturally, anxiety and concern took over, and I became preoccupied with trying to answer the unanswerable question: "Where will all of this lead?" I worried that my relationship with my son could become tenser.

If I could understand that he — and really all of us — is a mix of *tohu va'vohu* alongside order and clarity, I might be able to deal with his behavior more calmly. I might even welcome it and say to myself (and even to him), "He is a whole person with lots of different parts. How interesting! Let me ride this new wave of how he is presenting himself to us. I'm grateful that he's showing me."

We have all been, at one point, one of those parents for whom every problem needs to be met with a solution from a consultant or specialist. In our culture, we overdiagnose. We give our children the illusion that everything can be cured. We rush to intervene. In doing so, we deny two aspects of who our children are: They are kids who grow and change. Their developmental stages won't last forever.

Each child is unique. Each one has a unique personality and set of sensitivities that will grow and evolve but probably never completely disappear (nor would we want them to).

Tohu va'vohu can become a code phrase for the sense of chaos that accompanies each child's new developmental stage. We can be so concerned with — and, if we admit it to ourselves, even afraid of — each stage that we are not willing to let our children experience their own growing pains. The boy who clings to his mother every morning before entering his classroom does so because he experiences anxiety at his new school. He will feel calmer at some point, and he will enter the classroom on his own! The girl with high-pitched screams, demanding to be the center of attention, will eventually learn to share airtime at home. Most likely, they will "grow out of it."

Of course, there are situations with our children that require our attention, intervention, and expert guidance. The wisdom lies in knowing the difference.

Chaos as a Precondition of Creativity

Parker Palmer writes beautifully about the connection between chaos and order. Our initial impulse as parents is "to organize and orchestrate things so thoroughly that messiness will never bubble up around us and threaten to overwhelm us." But, as Parker reminds us, "chaos is the precondition to creativity: as every creation myth has it, life itself emerged from the void. Even that which has been created needs to be returned to chaos from time to time so it can be regenerated in more vital form."[1] Chaotic feelings are inherent in any creative process. Each child, parent, and family will inevitably go through periods that are dark and murky. This chaos is okay and even sometimes necessary so that something new can emerge.

---

1. Parker J. Palmer, *Let Your Life Speak: Listening for the Voice of Vocation* (Hoboken, NJ: John Wiley & Sons, 2000), 7.

Ayeka
Workbook

 Where are you — Ayeka? — in responding to the inevitable chaos of family life?

 Imagine you appreciated chaos and **tohu va'vohu** as part of the creative process of growth. How do you imagine responding to your children differently?

 What is holding you back from responding this way?

 Consider writing a mantra to remind yourself to embrace — and even bless — the chaos.

Living with Chaos

One afternoon, my husband came home from grocery shopping soon after our cleaner had just left. I was feeding my youngest, Shalva, a bowl of quinoa and, of course, these little kernels of superfood don't stay neatly in a bowl, especially when handled by a kindergartener. The quinoa ended up all over our newly washed floor. My husband was annoyed, and I was too. "But really," I muttered under my breath, "should the child only eat neat cheese sticks on the day the cleaner comes?" Leon quixotically hopes the floors will stay spotless for the week. I remind him that cleaning is really just maintenance to avoid the inevitable buildup of debris produced by our family of five.

As it turns out, our obsession with tidiness might have more serious implications than we realized. We do a fair share of hosting. My children have recently declared, "No little kids are allowed!" As they put it, little kids just make too much of a mess, especially in their rooms (!). I realized that this new stance is a direct reflection of us. Though we successfully communicated our desire to keep things neat and tidy at home, this might prevent them from cultivating new relationships, and may even get in the way of their learning true hospitality.

With the greater goal of generosity in mind, we now try to remind ourselves that quinoa can always be swept up and toys can always be put away. This small reminder can settle the rising feelings of momentary outer chaos and refocus us on the deeper feelings of calm that come from living generously.

How Am I Called to Respond?

The Hasidic masters interpret the human condition as a cycle: we fall, we get up, and we continue walking.[2] The formula is simple but incredibly reassuring. When we are down, when things feel out of control, we need to believe in the possibility of movement and change. When things are in order and under control, we need to accept that, inevitably, everything will return to disorder every now and again.

Any time we are stopped in our tracks or feel ourselves to be in a chaotic place, there is an opportunity for us to ask ourselves, "Where am I? (*Ayeka?*) How am I being called to respond to this challenging situation?" The question is equally valid for

2. I learned this in Rute Yair-Nussbaum's class on Hassidut, December 27, 2017. The teaching is based on Rebbe Nachman of Breslov and taught by her teacher Rabbi Shlomo Carlebach, who formulated the idea as this: "Human beings fall, rise, stand, and continue to walk."

more orderly, more harmonious, and calmer periods. Here, too, we must ask ourselves, "How am I being called to respond?"

Dwelling in the chaos is not at all easy. When my daughter yells, my ears hurt. When my son starts adolescence on the early side, my insides rattle. When my house is a mess, I get agitated.

Getting comfortable with chaos is not simple. But beginning to understand chaotic feelings as part of a necessary cycle — and having faith that this stage, too, will yield something important — is a key to growth.

8
Emotional Overload
An Opportunity to Respond with Deep Presence

In one of our Becoming a Soulful Parent groups, one mom told me, "It is literally impossible for me to be present. There is just too much happening in my life." We were sitting in the multipurpose room of a small synagogue in the Berkshires. The wood paneling and the hum of the heater created a cozy atmosphere for our gathering. I had prompted participants to share how they could cultivate more presence with family members, and to pair off to sound out their ideas in "spiritual *chevruta*" (paired learning). The rule of spiritual *chevruta* is to listen openly — without judging or giving advice. It's participants' favorite part of the program, in part because it's so rare to receive another person's full attention.

As we split off into pairs and my study partner began to share, I felt myself turning judgmental for the first time in my journey of facilitating these groups. I was *dying* to give her advice. She was a senior executive at a large company and full of frenetic energy. She spoke feverishly about her recent divorce, the dilemmas she faced with her teenage daughters, and her next executive meeting. Her mind was everywhere. I wanted to shout to her, "Slow down! Take a deep breath!

Your life is so filled with blessings! Take a moment to become aware of it all!"

As she spoke, I assured myself that I am nothing like her:

My kids are little.

I am married.

I work as an educator.

I was wearing a red sweater and hers is blue...

Ummmm.

Okay, I am exactly like her. We probably all are.

My unvoiced advice to her was really advice to myself. My mind is scattered everywhere. Since beginning to write this chapter, I have checked my email four times, composed a grocery list, and planned out how to respond to a work colleague.

Most of us are distracted most of the time. We are in a state of continuous "partial attention."[1]

This is a problem because no two moments are the same. Each moment has its own unique qualities, its unique feeling. When we miss the present moment, we are missing our lives.

As a culture, we are experiencing an attention deficit disaster. We are being called, beckoned, all the time to be elsewhere. The larger problem is that attention is the bedrock of learning and relationships. When we pay attention, we become more robust, centered, and grounded. Working on bringing back our attention when it drifts is the building block for everything else; especially for the relationships that

---

1. A term coined by Linda Stone, writer, speaker, and consultant. See her website, lindastone.net, accessed April 28, 2020, https://lindastone .net/qa/continuous-partial-attention/.

mean the most to us.[2] But when we don't pay attention, our relationships suffer.

The masters of distraction are our mobile devices. They beep and ping and light up and vibrate 24/7, reminding us that there is somewhere else, something else that we could be doing, right now — all the time. They divide our attention.

This kind of multitasking has trade-offs. It gives us something *fast*, says Dr. Micah Goodman, a contemporary Israeli thinker.[3] It gives us access, connection, the feeling that we are needed, and even an avenue for escape, especially when the thing we are experiencing feels boring, repetitive, or unengaging. But our devices take something from us as well: they take away something that is *slow*. They take away our ability to focus on any one thing. While we are always available, we can never give our full attention to any one activity. Our ever-present sense of distraction also makes us less able to deeply understand an issue. We run to quick fixes. We cannot stay anywhere long enough to grasp what lies beneath the surface of an important conversation, a predicament, a relationship, or an encounter with our children.

---

2. But hope is not lost, says neuroscientist Richard Davidson, since we are finally waking up to how inattentive we have become. Quoting psychologist William James, Davidson says, "The faculty of voluntarily bringing back a wandering attention, over and over again, is the very root of judgment, character, and will." Richard Davidson, "The Four Keys to Well-Being," *Greater Good Magazine*, March 21, 2016, https://greatergood.berkeley.edu/article/item/the_four_keys_to_well_being.

3. From a talk by Michah Goodman, the Jewish philosopher and writer, at the Keshet Talpaz school in Jerusalem in February 2019.

The Jewish philosopher Rav Shagar[4] addresses the root of multitasking's appeal: It is hard to "shrink" ourselves and be certain that *one particular thing* is what we should be doing; it is easier to allow ourselves to continually live in the vast world of possibilities.

> The human being lives always with a sense of running out of time. It is difficult to contract endless possibilities. There is a sweetness in allowing for boundless potential. There is never a perfect choice. There is an inner fear and trembling over choosing one option and having to live with that choice. It is always preferable to "sit on the fence," preserving an abundance of opportunities.[5]

Being connected to everything is the ultimate expression of FOMO (fear of missing out). Though our devices connect us to *everything* around us, they tend to pull us away from what is right in front of us.

How did this happen? It happened because we have turned time into a bully.[6] Time keeps us in line. It controls us. When we don't abide by its rules, it punishes us: "You didn't get that done, did you?" "You were late to that thing again, right?" How can we begin to orient ourselves differently toward time? If time is a construct, perhaps the "time crunch" we experience

---

4. Rabbi Shimon Gershon Rosenberg was a Torah scholar and a religious thinker whose thought was characterized by neo-Hasidism and postmodernism.

5. Rav Shagar, *Closing the Gate* (Efrat, Israel: Institute for the Advancement of Rav Shagar's Writings, 2011), chap. 1. Quoted in Ben David, *Becoming a Soulful Educator*, 54.

6. "The Inner Landscape of Beauty," *On Being*, last modified August 31, 2017, https://onbeing.org/programs/john-odonohue-the-inner-landscape -of-beauty-aug2017/.

is a construct too. Can we choose to do less sometimes and focus our attention more on what matters most to us?

It's Hard to Stay Focused

Focused attention can be a rare commodity in our home.

While sitting around the dinner table, my daughter Shalva has been known to reprimand me: "Don't speak with your mouth full, Imma!" Thank you, Miss Manners! But how can I not? There is so much happening around me. So many urgent questions seem to need my immediate response. During our family's rush hours of 7 a.m. and 5 p.m. (which I also call "bed, bath, and beyond"), I am in first-responder mode. It seems almost impossible to give my attention fully to any one thing. Or child. Or interaction.

I find Linda Stone's analysis particularly compelling. A writer and consultant on psychophysiology and our relationship with technology, Stone writes about the impact of our wired lives on our attention. We live with an "artificial sense of crisis," she writes. "We are always on high alert . . . we are reaching to keep a top priority in focus, while, at the same time, scanning the periphery to see if we are missing other opportunities. Our very fickle attention shifts focus. What's ringing? Who is it? How many emails? What's on my list?"[7] And while we are checking things off of our lists and getting things done, Stone continues, "the 'shadow side' of complex multi-tasking is over-stimulation and lack of fulfillment."

Stone's analysis of the digital world can be easily applied to our home lives too. For me, "high alert" mode begins in the

---

7. Linda Stone, "Beyond Simple Multi-tasking: Continuous Partial Attention," lindastone.net, November 30, 2009, https://lindastone .net/2009/11/30/beyond-simple-multi-tasking-continuous-partial -attention/.

evening. My kids are real extroverts. The more interaction, the more energy — and the more conflict — the better. The sound volume at bedtime is high. I often pantomime turning a dial with my hand: "Turn the volume to l-o-w, p-e-o-p-l-e!" Sometimes I wonder with exasperation, "When will they finally fall asleep? I need some quiet."

Everything, however, is in the present moment. "When a person does anything wholly," says Rav Abraham Isaac Kook, "whether in thought or in deed, they should rejoice and not do any other thing, because the whole world unfolds before them in that specific action." Instead of thinking, "Let's get through this already so that I can move on to X . . ." Rav Kook invites us to reorient ourselves, telling us to sink into this moment, this interaction, this conversation. After all, this interaction is *your whole world* right now.[8]

I recite the mantra "This moment, my whole world" in the most mundane moments with my kids. When I sit with Yael as she dives into her homework, I try to stay seated and not rush to fold laundry. This child. This moment. My whole world. What opens up for me when I am able to stay put is to marvel at her and how her mind works. When I rush to do something else, I miss that. On cue, Shalva seems to bounce into the room with her curly hair and dramatic flair and interrupts her sister and my focused attention. My blood pressure rises and I poise myself, ready to intervene. But I stop and say to myself, "This, this vying for attention, is also my whole world."

---

8. Abraham Isaac Kook, *Musar Avicha* 2:2.

Ayeka Workbook

On a scale of 1 to 10, how distracted are you when it comes to spending time with members of your family?

Name a family member to whom you give less attention.

What is one small step you can take toward becoming more present with that family member?

Each Moment, a World

Rav Kook taught us to be aware that each moment contains a whole world. The Hasidic masters add another dimension to our concept of presence — each moment *requires* something important of us: "Every *now* and its work."[9]

In other words, instead of asking, "How can I get through this moment?" the question we *should* be asking is: "What am I meant to do within the present moment? What is the particular way in which I, a unique individual, am meant to respond to this unique moment?"

There are so many reasons we may not want to be present in the moment. We might be physically or emotionally uncomfortable. We might feel drained or annoyed by what we are doing, thinking, "I'd rather be somewhere else or doing something

9. Rebbe Yitzchak Meir Alter, *Chidushei HaRim*, chap. 1.

else." Our experience might trigger an unpleasant emotion.

But when I see each moment as an active call, I can embrace the present, knowing there is something in it to help me evolve into a fuller person. As Shalva bounces in and interrupts time with Yael, I know my work in the moment is to stay calm, offer her a hug, and ask her to wait. I will turn my attention to her soon.

Spiritual Practices for Cultivating Presence

While many of us may have honed our ability to focus our attention via mindfulness exercises, deep breathing, visualization, meditation, or yoga, I'd like to revisit an ancient practice that can open us up in a different way — blessing.

Reciting blessings is a way of actively affirming every moment as necessary, real, and true. Each blessing is a response to what we see and experience around us. Blessings can help us pause and appreciate what we have (as when we offer a blessing over the food we eat). They can also help us link the present moment to the future (such as the tradition of blessing our children on Friday nights, in which we can articulate our hopes for them).

Blessing the Good and the Bad

Another type of blessing helps us to see the Divine in every moment of our lives — big and small, light and shadow. Imagine saying a blessing when you bought new furniture or saw the sea for the first time. Now imagine saying a blessing when you heard bad news or when your child failed a test. The Talmud tells us to say one hundred blessings every day. Even more remarkable is the Mishnah's assertion that "a person is obligated to bless the bad just as a person blesses the good" (Berakhot 9:3). Our days are filled with good and bad events that are part of our lives and our children's lives. Both types of moments are necessary to keep the world going. We can't spend our lives just waiting to get to the "good stuff," skipping what we view as "bad." If we can invest our presence equally in moments of light and shadow, we will not only move through our lives but also be moved by them too.

The Mishnah goes deeper, urging us to bless the *good that is in the bad* and the *bad that is in the good*. For me, this lesson feels most relevant in the context of my dual role as mother and daughter — I'm a card-carrying member of the sandwich generation.

My mother is not well. She lives with a nonmalignant brain tumor that has rendered three of her limbs immobile. A heavy cocktail of medication has made her drowsy on and off, and a recent break in her foot has kept her in bed. She is most alert, alive, and present when her grandchildren come through the door. She gives them her attention and focus as if they are the only people in the world, quieting her own thoughts and insecurities about what the future holds for her. I have noticed how she epitomizes Rav Kook's invitation to pay attention only to the current moment. The whole world unfolds for her when she is with them.

When it's just me and her, our time together is more challenging, less joyful. It is work to hold her, distract her, chat with her, and let her cry. Knowing our time together is limited, this time is worthy of so much blessing.

Ayeka
Workbook

 When are you most inspired to bless the good things in your life?

 Think about something that is not going well. If you were to offer a blessing for that situation, what might it be?

 Write a mantra for yourself to help you bless the good within the more challenging situations of your life.

9

Shabbat
The Entrance of Soulful Time

The room was small and the lights were dimmed. The Turkish floor tiles reverberated with our voices. We sat there — eight students — in the middle of the week and in the middle of our lives. Some of us were parents. Some of us were grandparents. We were calm, open, and ready to learn from our teachers how to renew our celebration of Shabbat at this stage in our lives. This class — which combined Jewish texts, poetry, and singing — was a perfect antidote for our spiritual life crisis.[1]

I was certainly ready.

You see, I used to *love* Shabbat.

In my twenties I came to Jerusalem and began to develop a robust religious and spiritual life. As the sun set on Friday nights, I would set off to the neighborhood synagogue, my heels clicking on the stones of a city paved with prayers. The little *shteibl* — with its simple plastic chairs, bare walls, and curtain separating men from women — was an environment in which I thrived. The sway of these prayerful women and men invited

---

1. Many of the insights in this chapter are gleaned from Dr. Elie Holtzer's singing workshop "Mizmor Shir L'Yom Hashabbat" on December 26, 2018.

me to join. The clear, focused belief of these Shabbat observers drew me in. My spiritual imagination took hold and I began to see the world differently for one day a week. This was not just Friday night; this was a day blessed by God and proclaimed as holy. On my walk to Friday-night dinner, the air was fresher. The food on Shabbat tasted better. My interactions with friends were deeper, more real. My hectic to-do lists faded into the week that was behind me; my task on Shabbat was simply to be. If I had been anxious about something during the week, I would kindly tell the thought, "You will need to wait. I will come back to you when Shabbat is over." Week after week, I practiced entering this mindset. "The Sabbaths," as Rabbi Abraham Joshua Heschel writes, "are our great cathedrals."[2] Nothing could penetrate them for me.

Except, of course, for kids. They can penetrate anything.

When our son, Tamir, first entered the scene, there was a sweetness in our emerging Shabbat traditions. I was hyper-intentional about incorporating child-focused rituals in our family's experience of Shabbat. We blessed Tamir with the traditional Hebrew blessing invoking the names of biblical forefathers whose qualities we hoped our new child would emulate. We sang Shabbat melodies in his ear, hoping that as he grew older and as our Shabbat table expanded to seat our future children, we would sing along to the melodies from their schools and hear their ideas about the *parasha* (weekly Torah portion). I fantasized about the emotional connection built on the exchange of ideas and stories.

My image at the time of how Shabbat *should* look is very far from my reality today. As the sun sets on Friday night, my

2. Abraham Joshua Heschel, *The Sabbath: Its Meaning for Modern Man* (New York: Farrar, Strauss and Giroux, 1979), 8.

children's decibels seem to amplify. They fight. They wrestle. In the meantime, my husband and I often quarrel. He is too strict for my taste (demanding that the kids come and sit at the table, *now!*) and I am too lenient (let's just chase after them until we catch them and then do that whole "blessing of the children" thing).

Shifting into a soulful mindset takes Herculean effort. All we can really hope for is to make it through our Shabbat dinner and the hours that follow in one piece.

And while we will try to correct our mistakes, set a new plan in place, and pray for our extroverted and very excited children to settle down long enough to enjoy the chicken soup, sometimes I feel as if I am *going through the motions* of Shabbat observance, waiting for my kids to get older so I can invite them back as grown-ups — when Shabbat will become real again.

Welcoming Shabbat and a New Perspective

Shalom aleichem — "Peace be upon you."

It's the greeting, the salutation, that we extend to Shabbat angels as we assemble around the Shabbat table. We invite these angels into our homes every Shabbat evening. They are messengers from another place; God's emissaries in this world.

For children, angels are real. But we grown-ups usually find it harder to talk about angels. Despite our disbelief, we may need to open our imagination to how angels can teach us lofty lessons.

We may imagine external entities, surrounding and protecting us. But angels can be found *within* us too. They can help us deepen our understanding of the world.

The Irish poet, author, priest, and philosopher John O'Donohue writes about angels in an aspirational way. In his poem "A Blessing of Angels," he writes of guardian angels that shelter us. Each angel brings a different blessing to enrich our lives. The "Angel of Awakening" invites us to become more open, to "come alive to the eternal" within us. Another angel, the "Angel of Wildness," comes to disturb us when we have become too complacent. This angel invites us to explore "the territories of true otherness" where we can make peace with "all that is awkward" in us.[3]

O'Donohue's angels invite us to view that which is "other" to us as an awakening, as a connection to something for which we may long.

The words of "Shalom Aleichem" can similarly evoke a new awareness on Shabbat. As I stand around my Friday-night table and start to sing, the angels I sing of are my messengers to help me experience and perceive things differently for this one day each week.

The song announces each stage in the angels' visit. *Shalom aleichem* ("Peace to you, angels!"), *boa'chem l'shalom* ("Come in peace, angels!"), *barchuni l'shalom* ("Bless me with peace, angels!"), and *tzeit'chem l'shalom* ("When you go, dear angels, go in peace"). However, another reading might go like this:

Hello and peace be to you, angels; *shalom aleichem*! Let me greet everything new that comes toward me — any new feeling, experience, or encounter — in peace. In other words, we are

3. John O'Donohue, *To Bless the Space Between Us: A Book of Blessings* (New York: Doubleday, 2008), 33.

saying you, too, are welcome here.[4]

Come in, angels; *boa'chem l'shalom*. Not only are you welcome here; please come into my innermost being. Reside with me for a while. Stay here for just enough time to help an extra soul, a *neshamah yeteira*,[5] take root in me. *Neshamah yeteira* is translated as "additional soul." (Beitzah 16a:12) The idea of an "additional soul" is derived from the phrase *Shabbat vayinafash* (Exodus 31:17), which I translate as "Shabbat and soul renewal." The Talmud understands the phrase to mean that an additional soul "comes down" to every person on Shabbat eve and departs at the conclusion of Shabbat. Others interpret it to mean that our heart expands on the Sabbath, or that our soul, which is shy during the week, is safe to emerge and take in life's beauty without being shouted down by the clamor and pace of our weekday lives.

Bless me, angels; *barchuni l'shalom*. Let me bless the possibility that I may see the world differently on this day, through the eyes of my additional soul. An extra dose of Godliness. An extra breath. Bless me that I experience time differently. Bless me to help me see myself, my children, my partner, and my home differently. Help me see the people and things most important to me with more love, compassion, and possibility for greater connection.

When you leave, *tzeit'chem l'shalom*. Help me bring a new perspective into the world, *my* world. Leave me with a *trace*, a *fragrance* of what I experienced with my additional soul on Shabbat, to carry into the week.

---

4. The statement is evocative of Rumi's poem, "The Guesthouse," *Rumi — The Book of Love: Poems of Ecstasy and Longing* (Athens, GA: Coleman Barks, 2002).

5. For more about the *neshamah yeteira*, read Rabbi Ilana Zeitman's sources here: https://www.sefaria.org.il/sheets/136683?lang=bi.

When I sing "Shalom Aleichem," I slow my pace a bit. I look at my family and savor them. The bouncing and wild behavior doesn't change much; they still spill grape juice on their white clothes, and I still ask them to sit through dinner. But internally I experience a slight shift. I open myself up to see them with new eyes — seeing my children's antics as part of their vibrancy, something to enjoy and relish. I put my fixed, judgmental voice to the side — the one that mutters "Why does he always have to act like this?" Instead, I connect with the imaginative possibilities of seeing the world through Shabbat eyes.

Ayeka Workbook

Read the full version of John O'Donohue's poem.[6]

Which angel would you like to receive into your life this week?

What small steps can you take to let that angel and the message it brings into your life even if only for a brief period? Try it for an hour or, for bonus points, a whole day.

---

6. Find John O'Donohue's full poem in *To Bless the Space Between Us: A Book of Blessings* or retrieve at http://mollystrongheart.blogspot.com/2015/01/for-new-year-blessing-of-angels.html.

Bringing a Shabbat Paradigm into Our Week

Shabbat eyes offer us a paradigm shift that we can bring into our parenting. Another such shift involves boundaries — specifically Shabbat boundaries. While I might regularly set boundaries for my children (all of the dos and don'ts of their daily lives), I am not too quick to set boundaries for myself. In my *external* life, of course, there are clear boundaries. There's the routine: up at a certain time, morning swim, getting the kids ready, off to work. Boundaries in my *internal* world are altogether different. It's not easy to focus on one thing at a time. The spheres of my life — personal, professional, and family — all meld together. While I work, I am also enrolling my kids in after-school activities and camp. While I am at home giving my daughter a bath, I am checking work-related messages. Though our fixed schedules give us the illusion that our time is designated for specific purposes (1 p.m. ... it's lunchtime; I must be hungry!), so much of our lives flow from one realm into the other.

Shabbat is commanded twice in the Bible: first, in the book of Exodus, as a part of the original pronouncement of the Ten Commandments; and second, in the book of Deuteronomy, when the Ten Commandments are repeated. The two instances differ in phrasing and offer us two paradigms of approaching Shabbat: *shamor et ha-Shabbat*, "guard the Sabbath day," versus *zakhor et ha-Shabbat*, "remember the Sabbath day."

The first paradigm, guarding Shabbat (*shamor*), is understood as an injunction to protect the character of Shabbat as a day of rest through *refraining* from certain universal acts of "work." This is the reason the rabbis prohibited activities such as building, farming, or writing rather than leaving the idea of "rest" to personal interpretation.

The second paradigm, remembering Shabbat (*zachor*), relates to all of the rituals we proactively *perform* on Shabbat to mark it as a special day. These include blessing our children and reciting blessings over wine or grape juice and challah.

But we can implement *shamor* and *zachor* beyond Shabbat. These two powerful paradigms can become mindsets to orient and focus our inner and outer lives:

+ *Shamor* — what do I need to keep out, keep at bay, or contain with a boundary so that it doesn't detract from my sense of presence or mindfulness vis-à-vis what is right in front of me?

+ *Zachor* — what do I actively *do* to celebrate and enhance my *time* (at work, with my family, or in my other relationships)?

Let's play with the idea for a minute.

At work, a *shamor* mindset would help keep me focused on my work tasks. When I am home giving my daughter a bath, I would focus my attention solely on her. And at mealtime — especially on Friday nights — what would it look like if I adopted a *shamor* mindset? What are all the don'ts that create a good, safe, and enjoyable space? Perhaps cell phones are not allowed at the table or insulting language is not accepted.

Then there is the *zachor* mindset. What are the "yes!"/ positive things we want to invite into the space of mealtime? Yes! — we can prepare food that everyone in the family likes. Yes! — we can share a highlight from our day. Yes! — we can have two desserts.

These two paradigms together form the shared mindset of *shamor ve-zachor* — we maintain a boundary to keep some things *out* and invite other things *in*. This can bring special meaning to our experience of Shabbat and the rest of the week.

Recently I facilitated a session about "becoming present." A young participant understood the concept beautifully. It is so hard to be present in our daily lives, she mused. But on Shabbat, the moment she lights her Shabbat candles — *poof!* — she is there. The two candles at the beginning of Shabbat and the braided *havdalah*[7] candle at the end of Shabbat create a boundary of light that says, "Now, in this twenty-five-hour period that has just commenced, practice just being *here* to celebrate." There are so many no's in traditional Shabbat celebration: no screens, no phones, no writing, no stressing. We need those no's so we can get to yes — yes to a day lived differently from the rest of the week; yes to a day of soulful living.

Boredom — Bring It On!

We spend so much time "busying" our children (with extra classes, sports, and after-school activities) that we cause them a lot of stress in the short term and a sense of unmooring in the long term. When they get older and begin college — and find themselves for the first time without a fully planned schedule — they can lose their way. When we plan everything for our kids, they don't learn how to handle boredom. But boredom is often the fertile ground from which creativity grows.

---

7. Traditionally, two candles are lit at sundown on Friday night to mark the beginning of Shabbat. At nightfall on Saturday night (when three stars appear in the sky), the *havdalah* ceremony is performed with a twisted candle.

The Jewish people's ancient answer to our children's growing stress levels — you guessed it — is Shabbat. It's a day to reorient ourselves from overstimulation to just the right dosage of stimulation; a day to reorient ourselves from a *doing* mindset to a *being* one. It's a day to observe the created world around us and not interfere with it. My favorite example of this reorientation is the rabbinic prohibition against picking a flower. Instead of picking a flower, we quietly observe it, beholding the world's natural process without changing a thing.[8]

My kids complain quite a bit about being bored on Shabbat. Soon after they articulate their feelings (especially if I don't get busy sharing all my great ideas for activities with them), they create plays, build forts, and find a nearby lap to sit on.

During the week, we not only keep our kids busy but we also give others carte blanche to influence them. They spend their days with teachers, coaches, tutors, and counselors. Shabbat, with less to do *by design*, can be a time when parents resume center stage as the main source of influence. For my family, one important value is hosting guests for Shabbat lunch. At our Shabbat table, conversation rolls into the afternoon hours, holding our children in a tight weave of community. For others, it might be sporting events, leisure activities, or nature walks. Shabbat teaches our kids that how we spend our time matters. What we choose to do together becomes their world.

I want Shabbat to help orient my own world. "Last in creation but the first planned,"[9] the sages teach. While Shabbat

---

8. Removing a plant from its source is considered akin to reaping, which is one of the thirty-nine categories of work detailed in the Talmud prohibited on Shabbat. For more details on this, see Mishneh Torah Shabbat 21:6.

9. "Lecha Dodi," liturgical poem.

was the last entity "created" in the creation story, the rabbis teach that it was preeminent in the mind of the Creator. While I feel the spirit of Shabbat settling within me when the sun sets every Friday night, its spirit of renewal is an opportunity I need each week — to remember how to slow down and receive the gift of connection to each member of my family in all their fullness.

10

Parenting Through Difficult Times

Cultivating Strong Souls in the Face of Extreme Challenge

When we experience difficult times (personal loss, natural disaster, war, or pandemic), our world is turned upside down. Any sense of order or control we think we have crumbles and family tensions can run high. When I think about how much strength parents need to summon to make it through each day during a crisis, becoming a soulful family seems like a distant dream. There are so many more immediate concerns to preoccupy us. Having soulful connections with our children is an aspiration at best.

Our homes can feel like pressure cookers. During difficult times, mine certainly does.

At the start of the COVID-19 pandemic, for example, that left us working and sheltering in place with our family for months on end, my husband, Leon, and I worked out an arrangement on paper in which we split the day. I work the morning shift (from 6 a.m. to 1 p.m.) and he works the afternoon shift (back home in the late evening). We thought that putting a schedule together would help us manage everyone else's schedules. Some days, my work time was interrupted with calls for *"Imma, Imma"* about one thing or another. Short fuses — and even shorter distances between us in our midsized apartment — gave us little time or space to figure out how to respond to everyone's mounting needs. The accusations from our youngest — "You don't know how to help me!" — and our responses — "Take a deep breath and we will figure this out!" — became our game of verbal volley during the daily homeschooling routine. Some days I got tired of playing and found my way to the garage, turning my car into a makeshift office for an hour or two.

Each family feels its own pressure, which boils and simmers over the weeks and months we live through any difficult period.

While COVID-19 is a recent example of parenting through difficult times, it is not the first, and won't be the last. During challenges that drain our precious resources, whether energy or time, where can weary parents turn for support and perspective?

Look to Our Elders

Our elders are our best guides to what it means to live a resilient life. They have lived through times characterized by great fear and loss. By their example they remind us that we don't choose *whether or not* to experience challenges in life but rather *how to move through* difficult times. They are, and continue to be, the best history teachers to our children.

Look Internally

Frameworks that support us in becoming soulful parents can help us get through any challenges. A sense of presence, the realization that chaotic feelings will rise and fall, is an important perspective to hold on to. Becoming attuned to each child's unique soul as a gift from beyond — with their own unique *tikkun* (repair) or contribution to the world waiting to emerge — can help us transcend the bumpy parts of our relationships that inevitably occur when things get tense at home. Recognizing our own soul qualities can be empowering and grounding. And being sure our children feel our love, even when they are driving us crazy, is the strongest pathway back to reconnecting.

Accessing these internal resources — our capacity to breathe and listen, our capacity to love and even expand our loving feelings during times of stress — and even trauma — can help guide us through interminable darkness.

Simple bids for connection with our children can have surprising results. A short bike ride with a child who is acting out can calm a difficult day. Entering the bedroom when your youngest is throwing a fit before bedtime and, instead of raising your voice, soothing her the way that only you know how, can settle them. Or staying in your ten-year-old's room listening to *his music* can ease the dynamics and communicate "we are in this together."

The systems we set in place at home can also create boundaries within which soulful connections can thrive. In my family, due to the recent COVID-19 outbreak we created "blackout time" from 6:30 to 8 p.m. every night to ensure there is an island of time away from screens and other distractions. In a flash their whole lives had gone online, and ours did too. We all needed the boundary to know that for a period of time each day, the whole world could wait. Creating blackout times communicates to everyone in the family that the emotional burden of living with stress is too much to bear alone, and that it can be shared when everyone is less distracted and more available. Once we set the rule at home, I found myself waiting for 6:30 p.m. to come, when I could just sit down for a minute and stop moving. This time now becomes a little island of Shabbat (day of rest) right there at the end of each day. A lull during an otherwise stormy time.

Ayeka Workbook

Think about a recent time in which your family experienced a great challenge (the COVID-19 pandemic is one example):

 Name one insight you've had about your life as a parent during that time.

 Name one beneficial practice that you began in your family.

What is one practical step you can take to keep that insight or practice alive in your family now?

Internal Resources for Children

It might take some effort — and even feel like *work* — for us adults to become attuned to our soul voices, to offer expansive love to those with whom we are closest, and to feel a connection to God. Children, on the other hand, come by these soulful qualities naturally.

According to Jewish wisdom literature, this connection actually begins in utero! A midrash (rabbinic writings that are part of Judaism's oral tradition) teaches that children possess a deep knowledge and connection to a source of light in the womb. According to the midrash,

> A lamp is lit for the unborn child above his head, and with its light, the child peers out and sees from one end of the world to the other end.... And the unborn child is taught the entire Torah. As soon as the child emerges into the air of the world, an angel comes and slaps the child's mouth, causing the child to forget the entire Torah. (Niddah 30b)

This midrash sets up a contrast between the inner world (in utero) and the outer world (ex utero, once they are born). It also sets up a contrast between knowing and not knowing. The central act of our lives is the process of recovering and reclaiming the intimate knowledge of the world that was once so close to us. Our children, who are closer in age to this source of knowing, can be our teachers. Lisa Miller, in her book *The Spiritual Child*, posits that spiritual sensibility may be inborn in all of us.

> Science now tells us that this spiritual faculty is inborn, fundamental to the human constitution, central in our physiology and psychology ... children are born fully fluent in this primal, nonverbal dimension of knowing.... Bird and flower, puddle and breeze, snowflake or garden slug: all of nature speaks to them and they respond.... Spirituality is the language of these moments, the transcendent experience of nourishing connection.[1]

Children are born with spiritual intelligence that can teach grown-ups a thing of two. While we usually rush by a ladybug,

---

1. Lisa Miller, *The Spiritual Child: The New Science on Parenting for Health and Lifelong Thriving* (New York: Picador, 2015), 26.

they stand fascinated by it. While we might dread another Zoom call with family members or another meal together with just the nuclear family, children are animated by these gatherings because they intuit that family time is sacred. Their enthusiasm for family and fascination with nature becomes the connective tissue to help them develop their inborn spiritual intelligence. By creating space to help them cultivate their natural spirituality, as Lisa Miller writes, "we can raise strong souls."[2] It is these strong souls who will have the emotional resilience to face the new reality that will emerge when the crisis is over.

Ayeka Workbook

 Think about your children. Name a time when each has expressed their inborn spiritual capacity.

Imagine that each child further develops that capacity. How might it help them get through difficult times?

 What is holding you back from helping your children cultivate those spiritual capacities?

 What is one (practical) step you can take to encourage their spiritual growth?

---

2. Miller, *Spiritual Child*, 132.

Viewing a period of extreme challenge as an opportunity for spiritual growth for both us and our children is not a simple matter. While the weight of a crisis and its impact on our personal, professional, and family lives feels crushing at times, there is always another way. That way is to remind ourselves daily, perhaps in the form of a prayer:

There is no "I" without "us."

Our breath is always there to calm and center us.

We can always tune in to a moment to be grateful for, however big or small.

We are all vulnerable, and our vulnerability is what makes us human.

Our elders are our best teachers. When we are stuck, ask them.

We are always in the process of becoming.

The Baal Shem Tov, the founder of Hasidism, famously said, "Let me fall if I must. The one I will become will catch me." With each challenge we face, wisdom literature can ground us, and the reflective time we give ourselves can help us explore our inner lives and grow in self-understanding.

11

Grandparents
The View Through
Love Lenses

As a young adult, I wanted to move as far away from home as I could. Don't get me wrong, I *love* my parents. But I needed to do what all young adults do — break away, become independent, and set up a life of my own. After I got married and started to raise a family, I wanted to move back home and be as close as I could. The move was tactical. (Can dear mom and dad please stay overnight so we can get some sleep?) Now, as my children grow older, what I need most is to see my children through my parents' eyes instead of my own.

You see, grandparents see their grandchildren through "love lenses," while parents see their children through "busy lenses." Love lenses see the children as cute, caring, and capable (which they are). Busy lenses see what is lacking: He must get better at math. She must learn to act like a mensch.[1] He must learn how to share.

A difference between parents and grandparents is that we see our children in "real time" and grandparents sees them

---

1. Yiddish for "man," used colloquially to mean "good person."

in "generational time."[2] Real time measures minutes spent on meetings with teachers, driving to activities, meal prep, and homework. Generational time counts decades; it measures the big-picture stuff, such as how long it takes for values to become internalized, for history lessons to impact today's decisions, and for wisdom from an earlier time to become an anchor for our families.

The real-time lens can be overwhelming. Whatever I am experiencing *now* with my kids, I project forward twenty years. I wonder to myself: Will she *always* slam the door to her room when she is upset? Will he *always* forget things? I feel a sense of urgency and pressure to address these issues immediately. Our parents, who more easily connect to generational time, can give us sorely needed perspective and help us slow down.

I must note that not all of us have good relationships with our parents:

They may have disappointed us when we were young.

They may continue to evoke cold feelings in us when we think of visiting.

We may feel their distance even when they are near.

Despite these feelings, it might be possible to view the ways our parents disappointed us when we were young with compassion. Perhaps they were overwhelmed — raising us in what was *their* "real time." Perhaps they were too preoccupied by their personal challenges to be fully present for us and our needs. Becoming curious about their lives and taking gentle steps toward reconnection may yield surprising results.

However, if you find your relationship with your parents too

2. America Ferrera, "America Ferrera and John Paul Lederach: How Change Happens, in Generational Time," *On Being*, last updated October 24, 2019, https://onbeing.org/programs/america-ferrera-john-paul-lederach-how-change-happens-in-generational-time-jun2018/.

loaded, or if your parents have passed away, I invite you to consider a different person who can offer wisdom and perspective the way a grandparent might. Choosing to actively cultivate a relationship *in locus grandparenti* — that is, grandparent figures who may not be blood relatives but live in our communities — might be an important and nourishing relationship for our children and for us.

Growing older is probably the most anticipated project of childhood. Every milestone is marked and celebrated: our child's first tooth, learning to read, growing tall and *finally* being able to ride that cool roller coaster. Around midlife we transition from "growing" to "aging."[3] As parents, we're in touch with both worlds. We are in close contact with our children: their struggles; their insecurities; and the new, intoxicating freedom that comes with their growth. We also care and feel responsible for our parents as they age and need our help.

We are the bridge between our parents, who carry with them so much history, and our children, who carry with them the potential to touch eternity. We are the portal through which their two worlds meet.

What would it mean to show up "soulfully" in that meeting place? What would it mean for us to consciously invite in the relationship between those who are aging and those who are growing, between legacy and newness, between history and eternity?

---

3. Adam Gopnik. "Practicing Doubt, Redrawing Faith," *On Being*, last updated December 7, 2017, https://onbeing.org/programs/adam -gopnik-practicing-doubt-redrawing-faith-dec2017/.

Ayeka Workbook

> If you could imagine a more nourishing relationship with your parents, what might that look like?

> What is holding you back from getting there?

> What is one small step you can take to improve your relationship with your parents?

> Once we imagine a more soulfully connected relationship with our parents, take the next step. Imagine you are at the end of your rope at home. What might your parent or grandparent tell you if they were right next to you?

Creating Soulful Intergenerational Relationships

Cultivating closer intergenerational connections may require an internal shift; it takes practice. Visiting our elders can feel like an obligation, a drain on our time and energy. We make polite conversation, we laugh at jokes that we don't find funny, and we ask how our parents and grandparents are, without *really* wanting to hear about the list of physical ailments afflicting them — maybe for fear that this will be us in thirty to forty years. Feeling awkward, we may count down the minutes until we can leave and resume doing what makes us feel comfortable.

For our elders, there may also be feelings of resentment or frustration, of feeling left out of family events or not valued for the wisdom and life experience they have to share.

There's a beautiful connection in Hebrew between the words for "agreement" (*amen*) and "practice" (*l'hitamen*).[4] When we say "Yes!" to something, we are also shifting our internal disposition through "exercise." If we agree that cultivating intergenerational connections is important for the health of our family, what are the *practices* of strengthening the relationships that grandparents, parents, and children can cultivate?

Practice for Parents 1: Putting Grandparents at the Center

There are many situations that are not only child friendly but also child-centered, with grandparents often relegated to the outer circle. "Grandparents need to be at the center," my wise-beyond-her-years rabbi, Tamar Elad-Applebaum, told me recently. We were discussing family-engagement strategies for our synagogue. "Grandparents are a testament to what it means to be alive," she said.

This philosophy extends beyond Grandparents Day at a child's school (which might have as much to do with next year's fundraising goals as it does with giving families quality time together). A grandparent's role is not only about kvelling over their grandchildren; the grandchildren should be invited to *kvell* over *them* as well.

Hasidic master Rebbe Nachman of Breslov reminds us that at the core of being human is falling, getting up again, and

---

4. From a *drasha* (rabbinic interpretation) given by Israeli Rabbi Tamar Elad-Applebaum, December 29, 2019.

continuing to walk. It is a sequence that repeats again and again. We experience setbacks. We fall ill. We have upsetting conversations. We experience rejection. To *agree* to get back up after each setback is worthy of honor. Our elders, by virtue of how long they have lived, have agreed to get up and continue walking over and over again. They are the ones from whom we need to learn. Those who have mastered careers, who have celebrated and raised families, who have suffered, and who have bounced back — these people hold the greatest wisdom for us.

If I'm honest with myself, I too am stuck in the child-centric paradigm. I showcase — and elevate to the heavens — every small thing my children do. In a Torah study class in Jerusalem last year, I remember speaking to my classmates with anticipation about the upcoming Passover holiday. One older person piped up, giving voice to what others were thinking. Eyes gleaming with indignation, she carped, "And then we have to sit around the Seder table, captive, and look at *everything* the kids brought back from preschool and pretend like it's the best thing since sliced matzah!" Lots of heads nodded in agreement. I shrunk down in my chair; she had exposed my own Seder plan!

My child-centered approach is also revealed by how I arrange my kids' time with their grandparents. In a recent visit with my parents, I came with a million ideas of things they could do with my kids.

I told my children, "They could watch you rock climbing!" "They could take you to the gymboree!"

Both my son and daughter (on different occasions) knew what they needed.

"That might be fun for *us*, Imma, but that's not us spending any *time* together."

Right.

Time. Together.

Time together is the gift they have with one another. With grandparents in their seventies, and all my children ten and under, God only knows how much time they will have together. (This is even more true of grandparents and grandchildren who live far away from one another.) With their simple logic and big hearts, they intuited that all they need is *time* — to feel their grandparents' love.

Practice for Parents 2: Creating Time for Storytelling

"Tell me more stories," my son asked, as he hopped into the car with his grandmother during a recent visit. It's one of his favorite topics of conversation. They've always been close. When he was born, I was shocked when I would *actually* need to get up in the middle of the night to take care of him. During her weekly visits, my mother would be with me in the small hours of those summer nights, her black and white *djellaba* loosely falling over her slight frame as she lulled my son to sleep. Many a sun-drenched morning we awoke to find him nuzzled next to her on the couch in the living room — a symphony of cotton pajamas.

My mother's presence has a magnetic pull. My son will run to her upon first seeing her, even though now she spends most days in a wheelchair. Her body is still a place of comfort in their prolonged hug.

Over the past decade, they have clocked good time together; she told him stories throughout. Now he simply recites these stories back to her. This child is comforted by knowing that what is true of him now was true of him way back then. His grandmother can capture his unique soul through the details of each story. Each story she retells him reminds him of when he was little.

One day he asked her, "When I was one and you would sing me lullabies, you were a little bit off key. I would correct you, right?" She answers, "Yes, honey, you have always had perfect pitch." The following day as we were traveling in the car with some of his friends, I asked my son about the anecdote he and his grandmother shared the day before. My mom was in the car too and she immediately shushed me. "These stories are just between me and him."

Stories create intimacy. They create connection. With each family story told, the storyteller recreates story lines, helps children better understand themselves, and gently strengthens children's sense of identity and belonging.

The connection between storytelling and identity formation has been the subject of much research. One study in particular explores the power of storytelling in children and teenagers. Dr. Marshall Duke and Robyn Fivush developed a tool in their Family Narratives Lab called "Do You Know?"[5] They have developed twenty open questions for children to explore with their elders because they have found that the more children and teenagers know about their family stories, the higher they will rate on tests measuring well-being.

As parents, we are uniquely positioned to evoke storytelling across the generations.

---

5. Robyn Fivush, "The 'Do You Know?' 20 Questions about Family Stories," Psychology Today, November 19, 2016, https://www.psychologytoday.com/intl/blog/the-stories-our-lives/201611/the-do-you-know-20-questions-about-family-stories.

Ayeka Workbook

 What stories do you retell about the relationship between your parents and your children?

 Think about a significant milestone for one of your children and share with them the ways in which their grandparents were present for them at that time.

Which new stories do you want to add to the family canon?

Practice for Grandchildren: Becoming Curious about Their Grandparents' Lives

I notice my parents don't tell so many stories about their own lives to my kids. But the few anecdotes they do share evoke and stimulate the sensory imagination. For instance, my father has a memory of his father washing his hands. It's a simple memory, yet it speaks volumes about how much my dad admired his father and his salt-of-the-earth ways. My father, now gray with age, still has a boyish manner. He laughs easily and heartily and has a mischievous glimmer in his eye. I am moved that all these years later, when I ask him about *his* father, he remembers himself as a young boy, standing at the sink to wash his hands before dinner, reaching his father's waist. His mother is wrapped, as always, in an apron, her thumbs blackened by the stain of the root vegetables she is holding steady, ready to be chopped. My father is positioned next to his father, transfixed by the steady stream of water and soap as it flows over those rough, wrinkled, and sturdy hands. He talks about these moments as ones in which he felt security and unqualified admiration for his father. As my father grew older and took over the family business, contention and healthy disagreement entered their dynamic.

The storyteller chooses which stories to tell, and the meaning is made in the telling. When my father shares these anecdotes, my children and I are transported to another time. A rich image of my grandfather emerges. I appreciate my grandfather differently now, years after his death. I didn't feel as if he really cared for children when we were growing up, and we weren't very close. My father's recollections are from the perspective of a young boy who adored his father and noticed everything about him. Our children watching us go about our daily lives will most likely remember these small moments too.

Ayeka Workbook

 Invite the grandparents to tell stories about their own lives as children.

 Invite your children to ask specific questions that evoke the color and texture of their grandparents' stories.

Practice for Grandparents: Becoming Curious about Their Grandchildren's Lives

"If I were drowning, would she get up and help me?" My daughter likes to put things in extremes. It's a way for her to ask, "How much does my grandmother *really* care about me?" My mother, who is mainly confined to a wheelchair, holds a love for her grandchildren that is boundless. Similarly, her attention and patience for them seems to never run out. She can watch them for a good thirty minutes as they methodically go through her wallet, taking out coin after coin, bill after bill, and rearranging all of her business and credit cards until they are in places she will never be able to retrieve them. "Aren't they adorable?" she will glow after each of these sessions.

"She would *want* to get up from her wheelchair, but she wouldn't be able to," I had to tell my daughter. Yael's real question, the one her seven-year-old self couldn't yet put into words, was something like, "If she really loves me, shouldn't the sheer power of love enable her to surpass her physical limitations and *do anything* for me?" Yael is our middle child. She is the child who wants to get as close to you as possible when you read her a book at night. For her, gravitational force is not a vertical thing but a horizontal one! You feel her love for you, and she expects to feel yours for her.

How can grandparents help their grandchildren *feel* their love (even when presents, treats, and special events reach their limit)? Inviting the grandparents to become curious about the inner lives of their grandchildren can be a good place to start.

During my parents' last visit, Yael was rattled by an experience she had outside her school. One adult was yelling at another and she was scared. Anxious thoughts kept rising for her, and she couldn't settle. I was quick to offer solution after solution. "Why don't you reframe it *this way* or try to think about it *that way?*" I asked her. She retreated slightly with each direction I offered. Her grandmother sat on the side, listening. She wasn't solution-oriented; she was Yael-oriented. My daughter could tell the difference and began telling my mother the details of the story she was carrying inside. Her grandmother listened with eyes alert and face open, welcoming any emotion or piece of information my daughter wanted to share. After some time, she offered up a few words: "I am thinking of a few ideas that might help you. But first, please tell me, are there any ideas that *you* think might be able to help you?" Her response gave Yael a chance to pause, take a deep breath, and process her experience the way she needed to.

This grandmother intuited the right pace. There was time. She gave attention. She was curious about her granddaughter's inner experience and gave her space to express it.

Ayeka Workbook

 Ask the grandparents to think about one thing they would want to learn about each grandchild's life in order to know them more deeply.

What questions would they want to ask their grandchildren? Ask them to listen without interruption.

If it is hard for grandparents to be fully present with their grandchildren, ask them to articulate what gets in the way of their being fully present while listening to their grandchildren. (Boredom? Busy? Physical challenges such as hearing? Other?)

Ask them, what's one step they can take toward overcoming what might be distracting them in order to stay fully attentive to their grandchild?

Crash Course in Emotional Intelligence Training

For many grandparents who live far away from their grandchildren, access to Facetime, Skype, and Zoom is a lifeline! These apps open up channels to see and experience their grandchildren for a weekly story hour, homework together, or just to say hi. Screen time can be the means to the greater end of fortifying the grandchild-grandparent connection. It is a silver lining in an otherwise gloomy forecast concerning the impact of screen time on our lives and relationships.

The preponderance of mobile devices and the rise in screen time for young people has precipitated a significant decline in empathy.[6] One way of thinking about empathy is "feeling with" another person. You can put yourself in their shoes. Through their facial expressions and body language, you can identify with their feelings. There is nothing that breaks that flow of "feeling with" another person more than an overdose of screens. Interpersonal connections, whether painful or joyous, become diluted once they're relegated to a quick text or WhatsApp message. When we avoid face-to-face encounters, we also avoid the demands that they present — namely, being fully present and vulnerable. We may choose to handle these moments that can turn awkward by quickly retrieving our devices.

When screens are taken away, we are left with the low-tech reality of someone's pain, sorrow, or joy. Inviting our children into contexts where they can experience these feelings — by the bedside of a sick grandparent, for example, or in a house of mourning after they pass — gives our children life's lasting lesson in being present. By letting children stay connected to their grandparents even as they age or become frail, grandparents can offer a lasting gift: a crash course in emotional intelligence training.

Jewish tradition has it that when a person visits someone who is ill, the visitor removes one-sixtieth of the illness (Nedarim 39a). When my mother was ill and bedridden, a visit from a

6. "Sherry Turkle: We Are Having a Crisis of Empathy," Children's Screen Time Action Network, October 31, 2017, https://screentimenetwork.org/resource/sherry-turkle-we-are-having-crisis-empathy.

grandchild brought her to life. Some children, who don't identify with the particularities of illness, can see past the pain to connect with the *essence* of the person before them. Their love can be blind. Bringing children into these contexts normalizes illness as a part of life and death — and illustrates how love endures through all phases of life.

For other children, encountering a grandparent who is ill may raise many big questions, such as "What happens if they don't get better?" or "Where will they go when they die?" While we might move quickly past these questions because we might not feel that we have an adequate answer, lingering long enough to be with them in their questions and their insights validates their experience and will help their inborn spiritual intelligence evolve.

Nowadays, in our COVID-19 reality, when in-person visits with our elders are severely restricted, videoconferencing on platforms such as Zoom has taken their place. Video calls present us with new challenges and new opportunities. On the one hand, it is so much harder for children to stay connected with their grandparents through a digital interface for long, especially when our elders are not able to play, respond, or interact readily. Still, inviting our children simply to be with, sing with, or even to breathe deeply with their elders can offer both sides a sense of presence that transcends conversation.

Children Offering Comfort After Death

It is customary for young children not to be present during *shiva* (the traditional seven-day mourning period) for a grandparent (as children bring joy, life, promise, and hope even when they are not intending to do so, and might distract the mourner from his or her feelings of loss). But what if we changed this practice and invited our children — *especially* those who are in elementary school and older — to experience this ancient mourning ritual? I believe that there are several lessons that can be learned from this.

To begin with, *shiva* can teach children that emotions are powerful and take a long time to process. We have a friend who didn't get to sit *shiva* after losing a close relative because her family doesn't believe in the practice. The three-hour reception at someone's home following the funeral left her feeling empty. She had so many memories to share. In what other context could she share them? The intensity of *shiva*'s seven days gives way to a less intense period of thirty days (called *shloshim*, or "thirty"), then the thirty days give way to an even less intense mourning period that lasts eleven months — a year of mourning in total. Loss takes time to settle. Allowing time for feelings to land and then go through a cycle is important to the healing process, and it's an important lesson for children too.

Another lesson to learn from visiting a mourner during *shiva* is that our emotional lives are fluid, not fixed. Sometimes we encounter a light feeling in a house of mourning that takes us by surprise. Delightful stories about the deceased, told with levity, are intermixed with sad moments, long pauses, and tears. Sadness and happiness can be held together. The *shiva* space can hold it all.

Finally, *shiva* is another way we can put the experience of our elders at the center. At a recent *shiva* for my own grandmother (who died at the ripe age of ninety-five), I was moved to see all of the elderly people who came to honor her. They shared their memories of my grandmother from a time long before any of us knew her. Along the way, they shared their own current health challenges and invited us to empathize with the fragility they experience now.

Our grandparents are our greatest teachers — both in life and in death. So many of us get caught up in the day-to-day tasks, joys, and struggles of being parents that we lose focus on what's important. Among all of this, connecting to grandparents can give us clarity. In the close view, our experience is like the tide — rolling in and out, constantly moving. But in the long view, when we cast our eyes toward the horizon, we see something steady and beautiful. And our grandparents see the long view. They teach us that what endures is connection: strengthened like a muscle, sinew after sinew, visit after visit. Invite your children, your parents, and yourself to practice strengthening this muscle, even when you may feel fatigued. In the end, this is the muscle that will last.

12

Prayer
Connecting to the
Need to Yearn

M y husband asks me the same question each time
I arrive about an hour after him to synagogue on
Saturday mornings: "How was it this morning?" The question
is innocent enough. He wants to receive a general update on
our morning's activities. Of course, I could meet his innocent
question with a generous and satisfying reply: "Good!" My
answer is to sigh and focus on my siddur (prayer book). I take
in the Hebrew letters: dependable, unmoving, unchanging.
I need their earthbound pull, the heaviness of ancient time, to
steady a morning filled with the dizzying motion of my children
spinning in their own vortexes and striking out at one another
every so often, just for the fun of it.

"Why do you guys fight all the time?" I asked Yael one Saturday morning. She looked at me with the grin of a preteen
slightly supersized on her young face. "Because it's fun."

Why can't a good old game of solitaire or reading a book be
considered fun activities for my three kids?

Our home can be a pressure cooker. On Saturday mornings
when we all begin to rattle, we just barely manage to zip, button,
and lace ourselves up and head outside for the ten-minute

walk to meet Leon, who has been at synagogue since its doors opened earlier that morning.

Here, in this sacred space, surrounded by white walls, smooth floors, and the friendly hum of prayers, the pressure is released and my children's energies simmer. There is space and light, and there are other children to play with.

Sometimes we get there late, "just in time" for the end of the service. On one such occasion, as members began to clear their chairs and prayer books, I clutched mine tightly. *I needed* to pray. And as my children and husband joined their friends at kiddush in the main hall, I left them and the general grown-up chatter and made my way to the back of the synagogue space. I found a quiet spot near the door that opened onto the green foliage of early autumn. I stayed put, the words and letters drawing me in.

"Instead of taking the words apart," I remembered theologian Henri Nouwen writing, "we should bring them together in our innermost being.... We should wonder which words are spoken directly to us and connect directly with our most personal story."[1] My eyes were pulled to the word *ahava* (love), which begins the prayer *Ahava Raba* (A Great Love). In the prayer book, this prayer immediately precedes the *Sh'ma*, Judaism's central declaration of faith. I started to play with the word in my mouth and was struck by the vowels: A-Ha-V-Aaaaaaaahh-hhh. There is so much breath in that word. It's a word that both starts and ends with *ah*. In the middle there is a *v* sound, *vet*. When you add a dot in the middle, the letter becomes *bet*. *Bet*...as in *Bereshit*, the first word of the Hebrew Bible: "In the beginning . . ."

----

1. Henry J. M. Nouwen, *Spiritual Direction: Wisdom for the Long Walk of Faith* (Grand Rapids: Zondervan, 2006), 92–93.

Over the span of that morning, I had sounded the first vowel *Ah!* with exasperation and was waiting for the *ahhhhhhh*, the moment of release. In the middle, *bet*, a new beginning, brought on by the prayer that entered me. The words *ahava raba* opened within me a new awareness, as if to say, "This Great Love of yours can hold everything. It can hold the *aaarrrgghhh* of the children's bickering and the *ahhhh* of tenderness too. It can hold the frustration and the release."

This prayer reminded me that even though I can shift quickly between frustration and release, I need to pay attention to the *bet*. At the climax of the transition — if I listen — is the chance for a new beginning.

Kiddush had ended; my prayer time was concluded. I took this insight, this new perspective, with me as I gathered up my children and we headed home into the autumn air.

Gaining Insight by Turning Inward

I invite you to pray — to pause and gain new perspective — by linking your personal story with an ancient one. My prayer space is often a synagogue, but your prayer space might be a mosque or a church. It might be the edge of your living room carpet, beneath a great tree in your backyard, or in your car before you go to work.

As Rabbi Abraham Joshua Heschel says, prayer is not suited for casual, occasional use now and again; "it is rather like an established residence for the innermost self."[2] Our innermost self needs a place away from the "falsehoods and absurdities"

---

2. Abraham Joshua Heschel, "On Prayer," Open Siddur Project, August 28, 1969, https://opensiddur.org/miscellanea/pedagogy/on-prayer-by -abraham-joshua-heschel-1969/.

of the world, writes Heschel. I would add that we also need a place away from the real and imagined concerns about our families that we carry with us: Am I doing okay as a parent? How are my children doing? Am I too strict? Not strict enough? Can I ever be sure?

I pray because my soul needs a home — a place in which to "simplify complexities, in which to call for help without being a coward. Such a home," Heschel states, "is prayer." How can prayer help us whenever we feel that we need to gather up our innermost selves, when we don't know what to do? Instead of seeking answers on our Facebook feed, we could incorporate into our routine the simple act of stopping our mad rush, offering a simple question in prayer — "What now?" This moment can often untangle the knot of worry that is wound tightly around us.

When I pray, I step into a different dimension, an internal quiet — *Ayeka* time par excellence. In this dimension, I don't feel obligated to answer the question, "What am I supposed to be doing now?" Prayer involves a different kind of probing. Prayer shifts the focus from *doing* to *affirming*. When I pause and return to my breath, or use ancient words to call out, I can connect to something far more essential — the knowledge that I have the internal resources to move through what I am experiencing. In fact, we all do.

No matter what our faith tradition, the opportunity for quiet meditation is ever-present. Whether they are words from the Gospels, the Qur'an, or our own heart, the practice of regular prayer opens a channel to connect to a spiritual life that can simultaneously elevate and ground us.

The traditional Jewish prayer book is filled with words. More and more words have been added over the centuries to this repository of generations of Jews who yearned for a connection to the beyond. These time-worn words of the prayer book can open doors within us.[3] When I utter them, I sink a bit deeper into my experience and feel something within me expand.

I chant the words.

I meditate on them.

I internalize them.

I try to live them.

My regular prayer practice is simple. At the beginning and end of each day, I chant *modeh ani l'fanekha*, "I am grateful before you, God!" This is the ancient formula for gratitude, meant to leave our lips each day before anything else we do. When I go to sleep at night, I say *Sh'ma Yisrael Adonai Eloheinu, Adonai Echad*, "Listen, O Israel, the Lord is God, the Lord is One," and I affirm that every discrete activity that happened during the day was part of a greater whole, or a greater oneness. That affirmation gives me a sense of calm before sleep. Each Friday night, as the sun sets, I light candles to welcome Shabbat, I whisper the traditional prayer while in my heart I pray to expand my capacity to cope, hold, and embrace my family *more*.

This meditative ritual, through its sustained repetition, powerfully reminds me what it is I yearn for.

---

3. I learned this way of thinking about prayer from Jerusalem-based Talmud teacher Rabbi Joel Levy, at the Maayanot Shabbaton in 2019.

Ayeka Workbook

 When was the last time you felt the impulse to pray? What were the circumstances of your life at that time?

 What word or phrase, if repeated over and over as a mantra, would give you calm, perspective, and a sense of direction?

 Start saying that word, phrase, or mantra, and be open to its impact on you.

Helping Our Children Pray

As parents, we want so much for our children. We want them to be happy, successful, and content. We want them to struggle and overcome; we want them to become resilient and kind. Do we also want them to develop a prayer life?

For some children, prayer comes naturally. God is an imminent presence in their lives. As a Jew, I sing the *Sh'ma* blessing to my kids at night along with another prayer, *B'shem Hashem*, which evokes the four angels to offer protection on all sides: Michael, the angel of protection, on the right; Gavriel, the angel of strength, on the left; Uriel, the angel of light, in front; and Shekhinat-El, God's presence, hovering above them each night as they drift off to sleep. When Yael was smaller, after I finished singing to her, she would sit up in bed and wave to each angel — "Goodnight, Gavriel! Goodnight,

Michael!" — wishing good night to each one in turn. Her relationship with the ineffable was innate. She felt the angels' protective powers surrounding her.

For other children, a relationship with God exists as needed, usually materializing around test-taking time. "Please, God, help me get 100!" The moment their immediate request is fulfilled, the impulse to pray fades. For yet other children, the idea of God is a fantasy; praying to something *beyond* seems ridiculous. "You know you are just praying to nothingness," I have overheard children say to their parents. They are working out what they think and believe.

Reciting simple prayers at night to thank God for the day's events, to open ourselves up to feeling protected or asking for strength to overcome difficulty, is common across faith traditions. Whether it's in the name of Allah and the Prophet Muhammad, Jesus, or the four angels mentioned above, the rhythm and repetition of nightly prayer helps settle children before bed, cultivate their sense of compassion and trust in something greater than themselves, and deepen their connection to the parents who pray with them.

Praying also helps children develop their internal spiritual intelligence — an intelligence that we might be less inclined to invest in compared to their logical, verbal, and spatial skills, but one that is just as important.[4] Prayer can help lower anxiety and depression. For our screen-hungry children, who learn to stifle uncomfortable feelings via the numbing effect of YouTube videos, prayer can help direct their gaze inward and bring them calm.[5]

---

4. Lisa Miller, *The Spiritual Child* (New York: Picador, 2015), 3.

5. Miller, *Spiritual Child*, 111.

Where Do I Begin?

One can start cultivating a prayer life with small steps. The first and most important step is simply *noticing*.

Once, on our way to school, with the hills of Jerusalem rolling past, I asked my kids to gaze outside. "Name three beautiful things you see," I said. They named the horizon, the way the clouds hung in the air ("It looks biblical!" my son added), and the green of the hillside. It was a spiritual version of "I Spy."

In an age when so many of our children's waking hours are spent gazing at screens, getting them to step outside of themselves and notice the world around them is already a great achievement. Asking them to offer thanks for the world's natural beauty can be the beginning of their cultivating a spiritual personality capable of prayer and blessing.

Ayeka Workbook

 Name three things that you are grateful for right now in the natural world.

 Ask your child to name three things that they are grateful for too.

 Share your gratitude lists with each other.

Imagine how your family life could be different if you take time to offer gratitude on a regular basis.

What's one small step you can take in that direction?

Cultivating prayer and noticing how much we are blessed can become part of a daily practice that gives us a moment to retreat into our inner sanctuary and soften how we relate to our families. The Hebrew word *brakhah* (blessing) contains within it the word *berekh* (knee). In the choreography of prayer, our knees are the flexible part of our body that bow low to honor something high. It's also the part of the body that can bend — that can yield and make way. When my reaction to my children's bickering is sharp, taking time to pray reorients my inner compass and enables me to engage with them in a more flexible way. To begin anew.

Afterword
A Love Letter

Dear Parent,

I want to leave you with a love letter. As with any good love letter, I hope you will return to this one again and again — at different stages in your life as a parent, partner, and human being. I hope that each time you read it, it will resonate with you a bit differently.

After all the anecdotes and guiding questions in this book, I think that becoming a soulful parent comes down to love.

It's not only the "Love you!" you might habitually call out when you send your children off in the morning and welcome them back at the end of the day. It's not the "I love you" you give your partner, with a kiss on the cheek, before rolling onto your side to sleep.

Love stands like a door at the entrance to our souls. Love can open spaces within us we didn't know we had.

Our love as parents is a demanding love.

It's an expanding love.

And it's always there, even when it feels distant from us.

It's a demanding love because it's *hard*. It's hard to love our children all the time, especially when the conditions aren't perfect. Because sometimes (okay, all the time) we are tired. Because sometimes our kids aggravate or even dismiss us. Because sometimes our partner doesn't appreciate us. Because sometimes we are not feeling in a generous mood about anything or anyone.

"Love your neighbor as yourself" is the well-known Golden Rule of the Mosaic tradition commanded in the book of Leviticus (19:18). Many rabbis have asked questions about this phrase. How can love be *commanded*? After all, it is an emotion. And what if I don't love myself? What if I don't love my neighbor? What if, sometimes, I don't really love … my kids?

The Hasidic master Sefat Emet shares an important insight on this. God would not command human beings to do something outside the realm of possibility. For example, there is no commandment to sprout wings and fly. If a commandment exists, it must be within the realm of possibility. It follows, therefore, that if we are commanded to love, it must be possible to evoke those feelings on demand. In the Sefat Emet's words,[1]

> Because the verse commands us to love, we must conclude that it is potentially possible for each individual to love, if only *he does what is necessary to arouse* this love [emphasis mine]. And this, in fact, is the essence of the commandment: that one should perform whatever actions are necessary to stimulate these latent feelings of love that are within.[2]

Essentially, the Sefat Emet writes, we are all capable of love, *even* when we are tired, aggravated, or feeling closed off from a member of our family. We each have the capacity to open up

---

1. Sefat Emet's commentary on Leviticus 19:18.

2. Translation from Ayeka's Soulful Educator Training Manual, 2016.

closed spaces within ourselves. Our work is to figure out what we need to do to *arouse* those feelings.

Easier said than done.

What kind of process might begin to arouse loving feelings? First and foremost, there is a self-care element. Let's get more sleep. Let's set ourselves better boundaries between work and home. Let's put our phones to rest for two hours when we get home in the evenings and mark that time as sacred for our families. (As you know by now, dear reader, I am not in the business of giving advice. Do what is right for you. But it can be helpful to take care of ourselves enough so that our general exhaustion and short tempers are not the main things our kids will remember about us. I remind myself daily to practice self-care.)

There's another part of this process. *Arousing* loving feelings is like exercising a muscle. Though I love to swim daily, I can get bored; staying in the pool for that extra ten laps demands effort. Nonetheless, I know that if I stick them out, next time will be easier — my muscle memory will kick in and my swim will flow better. It's the same with our families. Sometimes I just don't want to linger with my child longer at bedtime. (I've got stuff to do!) But when I stay, I am exercising my "love muscle" and arousing more care, concern, and connection with my child during the tender time before sleep.

Your children, partner, parents, siblings, friends, and everyone who is a part of the village that helps you raise your family are worthy of love, *by the very nature of their being human.*

Brené Brown succinctly shares this idea with a focus on children. She says, "All children are worthy of love and belonging."[3]

---

3. Brené Brown, "The Power of Vulnerability," TEDx Houston, June 2010, accessed May 26, 2020.

Rav Kook adds a mystical dimension: *"It is impossible for one to not* [emphasis mine] *be filled with love for every creature, since the light of the divine blessing shines in every thing, and every thing is the revealing of the beauty of God."*[4]

What if radical openness to love remained an aspiration for each of us? Sure, we might feel that some people are not deserving of our love. But what if we said yes more? Yes! — our parents, who are giving us unsolicited advice right now, are sharing something from their hard-earned experience! And yes! — our partner, who has a different way of seeing things, has his or her own soul and holds a good dose of blessing too. And even yes! — our child, who is acting dismissive, rude, or despondent, has the Divine within him or her. We can adjust our lenses in interactions with people we love, seeing beyond their challenging behavior to who they are.

Of course, we do not need to love or even *like* the bad behavior of those we love. We might experience rejection or residual feelings of resentment. We are always well within our right to say "No," "I don't like to be addressed that way," or "That is not helpful."

At the same time, we can also say to ourselves, "Yes! This person who is aggravating or acting in a disrespectful way — I still feel love for them." A change in the dynamic within our families can sprout, quite simply, from a fresh perspective.

---

4. Rav Kook, *Lights of Holiness* 4:389, 39.

Ayeka Workbook

- Write down one person in your family with whom you would want to cultivate a more loving relationship. What is getting in your way?

- What is one small step you can take to arouse your love for that family member so that he or she can feel your love?

While writing this book I have run several training sessions and workshops, bringing the Becoming a Soulful Parent approach and curriculum to leaders in communities and synagogues around North America. I am always struck by the dedication, willingness, and openness of the moms and dads who join the course to grow as parents. They want to become more present, more responsive, and more attentive to their children. What I have also noticed is that these moms and dads often have the hardest time being attentive to themselves. When I ask them to write down their own soul qualities and what makes them unique — their sense of fun, their sensitivity, how naturally athletic they are, their great storytelling skills, or really anything at all — their pens remain still in their hands.

Becoming a soulful parent starts with us.

Ayeka Workbook

 If you were to write a love letter to yourself, what would the opening line be?

If you were to write a love letter to yourself, what would the opening line be?

What moment or achievement are you proudest of as a parent?

What's a blessing you would give yourself to help you grow?

We are all in process. We are all growing. We are all doing what Lisa Miller so aptly calls "riding the tidal wave of love" and showing up, day after day, to greet the wave.

There are so many ways in which I want to have answers. I want to know that my children will be okay and will continue to grow into good people who contribute to the community. I want to know that all the challenges they face today may test them in the short term but will build their character in the long term. I want to see their challenges as opportunities for me to respond with compassion and love. I want to know they will grow up and strive to bring more wholeness to our world by offering the unique correction, or *tikkun*, that only they can bring.

Of course, there is a wide gap between my hopes and dreams for my children and the reality of today.

Today, there is a lot of homework to do.

Today, we need to figure out the right balance between time with friends and time at home.

Today, dinner needs to be made, eaten, and cleared away.

In these pages we focused a lot on the here and now. We focused on asking the question *Ayeka?* — Where are you now, today, as a parent?

The purpose of these exercises was to strengthen our soul muscles. Many of us might spend twenty minutes every day physically exercising our muscles for our body's well-being. In this book, each chapter encouraged us, through the lens of Jewish wisdom, to spend a period of time every day strengthening our soul muscles. We worked toward listening to our children with greater openness. We worked toward honoring differences. We worked toward ensuring that "I love you" isn't a pat phrase but that our children *feel* our love.

I pray that my soul muscles continue to strengthen over my life.

I pray that yours do too.

Love,

Dasee

Glossary

Abba: Hebrew for "father."

Ahava: Hebrew for "love."

Ayeka: Hebrew; literally, "Where are you?" This is the question God asks Adam in the book of Genesis after Adam and Eve eat from the forbidden fruit (Genesis 3:9).

Bashert: Yiddish for "fate" or "destiny"; often refers to one's "soul mate."

Beit ha-Mikdash: Hebrew; the ancient Temple that stood in Jerusalem and was the spiritual center of the Jewish people where the ancient Israelites offered sacrifices until its destruction by the Babylonians in 586 BCE. It was rebuilt in 538 BC and destroyed again by the Romans in 70 CE. Currently only the western retaining wall remains, which is a focal point of prayer and devotion for the Jewish people. According to rabbinic literature, the Shekhinah, or immanent aspect of the divine presence, is said to dwell over the area where the ancient Temple once stood.

Brakhah: Hebrew for "blessing."

Chevruta: Aramaic for "study partner." Learning with a partner is the classic Jewish style of study.

Dibur: Hebrew for "the spoken word."

Ezer k'negdo: Hebrew, often translated as "helpmate" or "help-meet." The word occurs in the context of God's search for a partner for the first human being, Adam (Genesis 2:18).

Hasidism: A Jewish spiritual revival movement that began in the eighteenth century in Ukraine. The founder of the movement was Israel Ben Eliezer, also known as the Baal Shem Tov, or "Master of the Good Name."

Havdalah: Hebrew; the Jewish ceremony of separation performed at the closing of the Sabbath after nightfall on Saturday.

Imma: Hebrew for "mom."

Kedushat habayit: Hebrew for "sanctity of the home."

Kiddush: Hebrew for "sanctification"; the ritual blessing said over wine on Friday night at the start of the Sabbath meal.

Kol: Hebrew for "voice" or "sound."

L'hitamen: Hebrew, meaning "to practice."

Mishnah: The primary collection of the Jewish oral tradition compiled and redacted by Judah ha-Nasi in 200 CE. It encompasses case law and various opposing views of the early rabbis.

Nekudah tovah: Hebrew for "good point"; used to describe someone's good characteristics.

Neshamah: Hebrew for "soul" or "spirit"; the word is based on the same Hebrew root as "breath."

Parasha: Hebrew; literally, "chapter." Used here to designate the chapter of the weekly Torah reading.

Pesach: Passover; the Jewish holiday of liberation that falls in the Hebrew month of Nissan and corresponds with the beginning of spring.

Pirkei Avot: Hebrew for "Ethics of the Fathers"; a compilation of ethical teachings found in the tractate Avot of the Mishnah.

Savlanut: Hebrew for "patience."

Seder: Hebrew; literally "order"; the festive meal and retelling of the liberation of the ancient Israelites from slavery in Egypt. The Seder takes place on the first and second nights of Passover in the diaspora and on the first night of the holiday in Israel.

Shabbat: Hebrew for "Sabbath"; the day of rest that takes place from sunset on Friday night through nightfall on Saturday. Jewish law mandates that no intentional creative work be done on this day. Instead, the day is spent with family and friends or in quiet contemplation.

Shalom: Hebrew; literally "peace"; used as a greeting.

Shalom aleichem: Hebrew; a formal greeting meaning "peace be upon you." This is also the name of a liturgical poem sung at the Shabbat table before the Kiddush.

Shalom bayit: Hebrew for "peace in the home."

Shamor ve-zachor: Hebrew for "guard and remember"; refers to the two times the commandment to observe the Sabbath is mentioned in the Hebrew Bible. "Remember the Sabbath day" is first mentioned in Exodus 20:7, while "guard the Sabbath day" is mentioned in Deuteronomy 5:11.

Shekhinah: Hebrew; the immanent aspect of God that, according to rabbinic tradition, "takes up residence" in particularly favorable situations (the term dwell is embedded in the word).

Shiva: Hebrew for "seven"; the seven-day period of mourning for a close relative.

Sh'ma: The fundamental statement of Jewish loyalty to God: "Hear, O Israel, the Eternal (is) our God, the Eternal is one." It is recited twice daily.

Shteibl: Yiddish for "small house"; a small and informal space for prayer gatherings, as opposed to a formal synagogue.

Talmud: The central body of work of Rabbinic Judaism from which Jewish law is derived.

Tikkun: Hebrew for "correct" or "fix"; evokes the story from the Jewish mystical tradition of repair that each person must take upon themselves to make the world whole again after the shattering of the vessels.

Tohu va'vohu: Hebrew for "chaos and emptiness"; the state of the world in Genesis 1:2.

Zemirot: Hebrew; songs generally sung around the Shabbat or holiday table. Many are taken from the book of Psalms.

About the Author

Dasee Berkowitz is a Jewish educator, facilitator, and founder of Ayeka's Becoming a Soulful Parent, a program that has inspired hundreds of parents and parent educators nationwide to bring soulful parenting to their families. Her writing has appeared in Kveller.com, Haaretz, the Forward, the Jewish Telegraph Agency, the Times of Israel, and other publications.

Dasee's work in creating meaningful pathways to parenthood builds on years experience in facilitating workshops and listening closely to the needs of parents and educators. She holds a master's degree in informal Jewish education from Hebrew University and a bachelor's degree from Barnard College, Columbia University, where she graduated magna cum laude. She has studied at the Pardes Institute for Jewish Studies and the Conservative Yeshiva—two experiences that helped her cultivate a unique pedagogical approach rooted in the wisdom of the Jewish tradition.

Dasee lives in Jerusalem with her husband and three children.

Acknowledgments

Each morning as I woke up to write this book, I reminded myself to stay focused by repeating "Give yourself this gift of time." It turns out writing this book was a gift that so many others gave to me and I am filled with gratitude. Thank you, first and foremost, to my own family. This book is a time capsule of our lives. Your generosity to permit me to reflect on these experiences openly is courageous and kind. To Leon, for being my *ezer k'negdo* who encouraged me every step of the way, challenges me to grow, and loves me fully. Thank you especially for your patience during my daily 5 a.m. writing sessions, which woke you up too. To Tamir, Yael, and Shalva, for your passion, tenderness, and strong hugs. You have helped me become a more loving, patient, and present mother each day. I love you up to the sky and back again, a million times over.

For all of the rabbis, educators, and parents who have led and participated in a Becoming a Soulful Parent group over the past five years — you have brought your full selves, openly and honestly, and have modeled for others what it means to become soulful people. Special thanks to the very first Becoming a Soulful Parent group in Jerusalem — to Lynne and Adam, Ilene and Nachshon, Dara and Robby, Jessica and Daniel, Bracha and Paul. Through learning and laughter you helped me work out so many of the ideas contained in this book. To Molly Brodsky and Maayan Rabinovich, who ran the first Becoming a Soulful Parent groups; and to Rabbis Jenny Solomon, Judy Kempler, and Bethie Miller, who have guided so many groups over the years. To Mark Horowitz, Mackenzie Adams, and Veronica Maravankin, you have championed the Becoming a Soulful Parent program, educational workshops, and network through the JCC Association since the program's inception. Your encouragement and care means so much to me.

To my teachers, Rute Yair-Nussbaum, Dr. Elie Holtzer, Karina Zilberman, Rabbi Tamar Elad-Applebaum, and Batsheva Sumet: your insights on Hassidut and humanity have inspired me to think more expansively.

To members of the synagogues where my family has found a second home over the past decade, Temple Adas Israel, Ma'ayanot, and Kehilat Zion: you have inspired me in so many ways.

To my friends and colleagues, many of whom read earlier drafts of the manuscript and whose wise counsel and clarifying questions gave me renewed energy to continue working. Meredith Lewis, Alisa Kotler-Berkowitz, Shira Lupiansky Hasson, Lynne Weinstein, Caryn Green, Yael Goodman Korda, Michal Smart, Judy Kupchan, Marci Bornstein, Dalia Hochman, and Gili Ro'i: thank you.

To my writing group, Rebecca Bardach and Julia Schlam, for our writing retreats, replete with so much coffee and chocolate, and for your encouragement to make writing our books a priority! And to the fine folks at the Tantur Ecumenical Institute, the Convent of the Sisters of Sion, and the Coffee Mill, where much of this book was conceived and written down.

To other dear friends, Noa Heyman, Andrea Hendler, Mallory Serebrin, Noy Mordekovitch, Daniella Yanai, Rhonda Adessky, Jay Kaplan, Jodi Sperling and Josh Kaplan, and Danny Hasson: thank you for being my source of deep joy and support over the years.

To my colleagues at Ayeka's Center for Soulful Education; Rabbi Aryeh Ben David, your wisdom, creativity, and guidance have anchored me since the conception of the Becoming a Soulful Parent program. A special thanks to the whole Ayeka team, including Rabbi Yehoshua Looks, Michal Smart, Clare Goldwater, David Kahn, Shira Stein, and Mick Weinstein, for being a constant source of support and encouragement. To Esther Goldenberg, for being an amazing book coach just at the right time; and to Sofia Freudenstein, for your skillful research. Leora Niderberg, your careful reading and precise editing graces each and every page. To Emily Wichland; you are a copyeditor par excellence! You helped us reach the finish line with ease and your impeccable skill.

And to Susie Lubell, for the beautiful cover artwork.

Thank you to Yael Shahar and Don Radlauer at Kasva Press for taking this project on with enthusiasm. You have been a pleasure to work with at every turn! And to the Beker Family Foundation for your partnership and support over the years.

To my family of origin: Mom, Dad, and Alisa, you are the examples of what it means to be soulful human beings. Your unconditional love, lessons about risk, resilience, and unending support continue to guide me, always.

Going Deeper

While I was writing the book *Becoming a Soulful Parent: A Path to the wisdom within*, I wanted to create a dance between stories and anecdotes in my own life and the stories that animate yours. The Ayeka Workbook questions invite each of us to move, step, or leap at our own pace.

But none of us parent alone. Friends, colleagues, and other community members share in our stories, successes, and struggles. So we have created some great resources to help you gather your "people" together to share:

- ✦ A Book Guide, which will include ideas for facilitating a group, along with excerpts from the book and other goodies.

- ✦ Meaningful activities to do with your children.

Check out all of these resources and more on the Soulful Parent wesbsite: www.soulfulparent.com.

About Ayeka

In 2006, after teaching Jewish texts to adults for twenty years, Aryeh Ben David founded Ayeka: Center for Soulful Education. Ayeka affirms that the goal of learning Jewish wisdom is to affect and evoke our better selves. To do this, we need to recognize that the mind learns differently than the heart, that learning needs to engage our souls, and that the ultimate goal of acquiring Jewish knowledge is to impact our everyday lives.

Ayeka developed a unique and innovative educational approach that enables us to bring Jewish wisdom from our minds to our hearts, to our souls, and into our lives — while honoring that every individual is on his or her unique path, at his or her unique pace. We are all works-in-progress, and Jewish wisdom can be the ideal guide on our journeys toward becoming our better selves. *"Ayeka"*, which means "Where are you?", was created to provide this opportunity.

What We Do:

Ayeka's program tracks include:

- ✦ Becoming a Soulful Individual
- ✦ Becoming a Soulful Family
- ✦ Becoming a Soulful Educator

In 2015, Dasee Berkowitz initiated the Becoming a Soulful Parent program to empower parents to become more reflective, and to see every challenge as an opportunity for spiritual growth. To date, the Becoming a Soulful Parent program has inspired other facilitators to run their own soulful parenting groups, which have impacted hundreds of parents.

Participants in all of our trainings, programs, and webinars include rabbis, educators, Jewish professionals, parents, grandparents, and individual learners from every background and denomination who want more; who want a method of engaging with traditional Jewish wisdom that enables them to clarify their own unique paths and purpose, and enhance their lives.

About Kasva Press

"Make its bowls, ladles,
jars and pitchers
with which to offer libations;
make them of pure gold."
(Exodus 25:29)

וְעָשִׂיתָ קְּעָרֹתָיו וְכַפֹּתָיו
וּקְשׂוֹתָיו וּמְנַקִּיֹּתָיו
אֲשֶׁר יֻסַּךְ בָּהֵן
זָהָב טָהוֹר תַּעֲשֶׂה אֹתָם
(שמות פרשת תרומה)

Kasva means "a jar or pitcher". The word appears in the Torah exactly once, where it describes the solid-gold vessels made to hold sacrificial wine and oil in the Tabernacle the Israelites carried with them in their desert wanderings.

We believe that a good book is a vessel for the fluid thoughts of its author — its words, the outpouring of the writer's soul, as precious as the sanctified wine and oil of the Tabernacle.

It is our aim to provide worthy vessels for our authors' creations.